Principles of Love

Principles of Love

Charles G. Finney

Compiled & Edited by
Louis Gifford Parkhurst, Jr.

BETHANY HOUSE PUBLISHERS
MINNEAPOLIS, MINNESOTA 55438
A Division of Bethany Fellowship, Inc.

Published by Bethany House Publishers
A Division of Bethany Fellowship, Inc.
6820 Auto Club Road, Minneapolis, Minnesota 55438

Printed in the United States of America

Library of Congress Cataloging-in-Publication Data

Finney, Charles Grandison, 1792-1875.
   Principles of love.

   1. Love—Religious aspects—Christianity—Meditations.
2. Love—Religious aspects—Christianity—Sermons.
3. Congregational churches—Sermons.   4. Sermons, American.
I. Parkhurst, Louis Gifford, 1946-   .   II. Title.
BV4639.F55   1986   241'.4   86-1078
ISBN 0-87123-866-7 (pbk.)

CHARLES G. FINNEY was one of America's foremost evangelists. Over half a million people were converted under his ministry in an age that offered neither amplifiers nor mass communications as tools. Harvard Professor Perry Miller affirmed that "Finney led America out of the eighteenth century." As a theologian, he is best known for his *Revival Lectures* and his *Systematic Theology*.

LOUIS GIFFORD PARKHURST, JR., is pastor of First Christian Church of Rochester, Minnesota, and teaches Ethics/Philosophy at Minnesota Bible College. He garnered a B.A. and an M.A. from the University of Oklahoma and an M.Div. degree from Princeton Theological Seminary. He is married and the father of two children.

BOOKS IN THIS SERIES

Principles of Christian Obedience
Principles of Consecration
Principles of Devotion
Principles of Discipleship
Principles of Faith
Principles of Holiness
Principles of Liberty
Principles of Love
Principles of Prayer
Principles of Revival
Principles of Salvation
Principles of Sanctification
Principles of Union with Christ
Principles of Victory

OTHER BOOKS BY FINNEY

Answers to Prayer
Finney's Systematic Theology
Heart of Truth, Finney's Outline of Theology
Lectures on Revival
Reflections on Revival
Finney on Revival
Promise of the Spirit
Autobiography of Charles G. Finney
The Believer's Secret of Spiritual Power (with Andrew Murray)

The Life and Ministry of Charles Finney / Lewis Drummond

CONTENTS

INTRODUCTION

The primary value of this new book in the "Finney Principles Series" is the careful combination within the same study of the appropriate attribute of love with its opposite, the attribute of selfishness. You will gain a clearer understanding of Christian love by studying at the same time what God expects us to do and what He expects us to avoid. Just as a specialist in rare coins carefully inspects both sides of a coin to determine its real worth, we are to find out what true love is by also knowing its opposite—true selfishness or self-indulgence. Finney's introduction to the study of these attributes has been combined from two lectures into "The Psychology of Love."

Principles of Love is a vastly expanded version of the material found in either *Finney's Systematic Theology* or *Love Is Not a Special Way of Feeling*. Taken from the first edition of his *Lectures on Systematic Theology* (Vol. II, 1846), more attributes are discussed than in the current edition of *Finney's Systematic Theology*. The attributes of selfishness are not included in *Love Is Not a Special Way of Feeling*. In addition to much new material, this book also includes three of Finney's best sermons on love from *The Oberlin Evangelist*.

I have added the Scripture verses at the beginning of each chapter as a key to the study of each principle of love. These verses are from the *New International Version of the Bible*. All other Scripture quotations are from the version Finney used in his *Systematic Theology*. I have concluded each study with a summary positive statement called "For Reflection." I hope you will read these statements and affirm them prayerfully for your own life. As you would expect, Finney's thoughts on love are deeply profound and demand your most intense thinking as you apply them to your heart. I strongly encourage you to read no more than one meditation a day, and patiently think it through before going on to the next one. Finney wrote to encourage us to think. With Jesus' help, you will begin to manifest His love in your life more and more consistently as you apply the principles in this book.

For the sake of His Kingdom,
L. G. Parkhurst, Jr.

THE PSYCHOLOGY OF LOVE

The sum and spirit of the law of God is properly expressed in one word, *love*. Love is benevolence or good willing. Love consists in choosing the highest good of God and universal being (everything God has created) as the ultimate end for its own sake, or because of its own intrinsic value. *Love* is the spirit or the state of entire consecration to the highest good of God and universal being as the ultimate end or ultimate purpose of existence.

Although the whole law of God is fulfilled in one word, *love*, yet there are many things implied in the state of mind expressed by this term. It is, therefore, indispensable for a right understanding of this subject that we inquire into the characteristics or attributes of love. At the same time, we must constantly keep in mind certain truths about mental philosophy or psychology.

Certain facts in mental philosophy are revealed in our consciousness. First, all moral agents possess intelligence, or the faculty of knowledge. Second, all moral agents possess sensibility, or the faculty of emotion. Third, all moral agents possess will, or the power of choosing or refusing in every case of moral obligation.

These primary faculties, which belong to all moral agents, are so interrelated with each other that the intellect or the emotions may control the will. Or the will in a certain sense may control the intellect or the emotions. The will is free to choose according to the demands of the intellect. Or the will may choose according to the desires and impulses of the emotions. The will is free to be influenced by feelings or by the dictates of intelligence. Or the will is free to control and direct both the intellect and the feelings.

The will can directly control the attention of the intellect, and consequently its perceptions and thoughts. The will can *indirectly* control the state of the emotions, by controlling the perceptions and thoughts of the intelligence.

We also know from our consciousness that the voluntary muscles of our bodies are directly controlled by the will. The relation of the outward actions of our muscles as well as the states of the intelligence and the emotions depend upon the action of the will by necessity. That is, the physical law, or the law of necessity, obliges the intellect, the feelings, and the actions of the body to obey the decisions of the will. The attention of the intellect and the outward actions of the voluntary muscles are controlled directly, and the feelings indirectly, by the decisions of the will. The will can either command or obey. It can allow itself to be enslaved by feelings or it can assert its sovereignty and control them. The will is not influenced by either the intellect or the emotions by the law of necessity or force; therefore, the will can always resist either the demands of the intelligence or the impulses of emotions. While the intelligence or the feelings cannot *lord* it over the will through the agency of any law of force, the will has the aid of the law of necessity or force by which to control them.

We are conscious of affirming to ourselves our obligation to obey the law of the intelligence rather than the impulses of our feelings. We know that to act virtuously, we must act rationally or intelligently, and not give ourselves over to the blind impulses of our feelings.

Since the love required by the moral law consists in choice, willing or intention, as has been repeatedly shown, and since choice, willing or intention, controls the states of the intellect and the outward actions directly by a law of necessity, and by the same law controls the feelings indirectly, it follows that certain states of the intellect and the feelings, and also certain outward actions, must be implied in the love which the law of God requires. I say implied in it, not as making a part of it, but as *necessarily resulting from it.* The thoughts, opinions, judgments, feelings, and outward actions must be molded and modified by the state of the heart or will.

Here it is important to remark that in everyday speech, the same word is often used to express either an action or state of the will, or a state of the emotions, or both. This is true of all the terms that represent what are called the Christian graces or virtues, or those various aspects of virtue of which Christians are conscious and which appear in their life and temperament. We shall be constantly reminded of this truth as we proceed in our investigations, for we will find illustrations of it at every step of our progress.

Before we discuss the attributes of benevolence, it is important to remark that all the moral attributes of God and of all holy beings are only attributes of benevolence. Benevolence is a term that comprehensively expresses them all. *God is love.* This term expresses comprehensively God's whole moral character. This love is benevolence. Benevolence is good willing, or the choice of the highest good of God and the universe as an end. But from this comprehensive statement, accurate though it is, we are apt to receive very inadequate conceptions of what really belongs *to* and is implied *in* benevolence.

To say that love is the fulfilling of the whole law; that benevolence is the whole of true religion; that the whole duty of man to God and his neighbor is expressed in one word, *love;* these statements, though true, are so comprehensive they need much amplification and explanation. The fact is that many things are implied in love or benevolence. Benevolence needs to be viewed under various aspects and in various relations, and its dispositions or willings need to be considered in the various relations in which it is called to act.

Benevolence is an ultimate intention, or the choice of an ultimate end. If we suppose that this is all that is implied in benevolence, we will greatly err. Unless we inquire into the nature of the end which benevolence chooses, and the means by which benevolence seeks to accomplish that end, we shall understand very little of the importance of the word *benevolence*. Benevolence has many attributes or characteristics. These must all harmonize in the selection of its end, and in its efforts to realize it. *Wisdom, justice, mercy, truth, holiness*, and many other attributes are essential elements or attributes of benevolence.

To understand what true benevolence is we must inquire into its attributes. Not everything that is called *love* bears the nature of benevolence. Nor has all that is called *benevolence* any right to the use of the term. There are various kinds of love. Natural affection is called love. The affection that exists between the sexes is also called love. Our preference for certain kinds of food is called love. We say that we love fruit, vegetables, meat, and milk. Benevolence is also called love, and is the kind of love, beyond all question, required by the law of God.

But there is more than one state of mind that is called benevolence. There is an innate benevolence which is often mistaken for and confused with the benevolence which constitutes virtue. This so-called benevolence is in truth only an imposing form of selfishness; nevertheless, it is called benevolence. Many of its manifestations resemble those of true benevolence. Care, therefore, should be taken in giving religious instruction to distinguish accurately between them. Benevolence, let it be remembered, is the obedience of the will to the law of reason. Benevolence is willing good as an end, for its own sake, and not to gratify self. Selfishness does just the opposite. It renders obedience of the will to the impulses of the feelings. Selfishness is a spirit of self-gratification, where the will seeks to gratify the desires and propensities for the pleasure of the gratification. Self-gratification becomes the ultimate choice rather than obedience to the claims of God and the good of being. Innate benevolence is only obedience to the impulse of the feelings—a yielding to a feeling of compassion. It is only an effort to gratify a desire. An effort to gratify any desire whatever, is really selfishness.

It is important to realize that the moral attributes of God, as revealed in His works, providence, and Word, throw much light upon the subject before us. Also, the many precepts of the

Bible, and the developments of benevolence within the Bible, will help us as we continue to study this important subject. The Bible expressly affirms that love embraces the whole character of God, that love is the sum of what the law requires of man, that the end of the commandment is charity, or love. We may be assured that every form of true virtue is only a modification of love, or benevolence; that is, every state of mind required by the Bible and recognized as virtue is in its last analysis resolvable into love, or benevolence. In other words, every virtue is only benevolence viewed under certain aspects or in certain relations. Every virtue is only one of the elements, peculiarities, characteristics, or attributes of benevolence. This is true of God's moral attributes. They are, as has been said, only attributes of benevolence. They are only benevolence manifested in certain relations and aspects. All His virtues are but the sum total of benevolence. This is and must be true of every holy being. It is essential for us, therefore, to understand the attributes of that love which constitutes obedience to the law of God.

In the following meditations, we will be comparing and contrasting the attributes of love with the attributes of selfishness. It is important to see how selfishness manifests itself under various attributes. By understanding what true love is in the context of its opposite, true selfishness, we will know if we are truly obedient to God.

Disobedience to moral law always consists in selfishness. Selfishness lies in the ultimate choice of our own gratification. An ultimate choice is a final intention of purpose, or the choice of something for its own sake or for its own intrinsic value. The choice of our own gratification as an ultimate end is the preference of our own gratification not merely because we see gratification as something good, but because we see and choose that gratification or good because it is for our own self.

Selfishness chooses and cares for good only upon condition that it belongs to self. It is not the gratification of being in general, but self-gratification upon which selfishness hinges. It is a good because it belongs to self or is chosen upon that condition. But when it is affirmed that selfishness is sin and the whole of sin, we are in danger of misconceiving the vast importance of the word and of taking a very narrow, superficial, and inadequate view of the subject. Because of this misconception, it is therefore indispensable to raise and push the inquiry, and compare it with true love.

What is implied in selfishness? What are its characteristics and essential elements? What modifications or attributes does it develop and manifest under the various circumstances in which we see it manifested in the providence of God. Primarily, it consists in the committal of the will to the gratification of *desire*. The Apostle calls it "fulfilling the desires of the flesh and of the mind." What must be implied in the state of mind which consists in the committal of the whole being to the gratification of self as an end? What must be the effect upon the desires themselves under such indulgence? What must be the effect upon the intellect to have its high demands trampled under foot? How is it manifested in the outward life? What must be the effect upon the temperament and spirit to have self-indulgence the law of the soul? This leads us to the investigation of the point before us—namely *what is implied in disobedience to moral law?*

Why is selfishness blameworthy? Why is a spirit of self-seeking in mere animals or brute beasts not as much a breach of moral law as is the same spirit in man? If the spirit of self-seeking in man is sin, what is implied in this fact? In other words, what conditions are necessary to render a spirit of self-seeking a breach of moral law? These conditions must be implied in disobedience to moral law.

1. Disobedience to moral law implies the possession of the powers of moral agency. Mere animals may do that which the moral law prohibits in moral agents. But the moral law does not legislate over them; therefore, those things in them are not sin, not a violation of the moral law.

2. Disobedience to moral law implies knowledge of the end which a moral agent is obligated to choose. We have seen that the moral law requires love and that this love is benevolence. It is the disinterested and impartial choice of the highest good of God and of being in general as an end. Now it follows that this end must be clearly understood before we can possibly choose

it. Therefore, obligation to choose it implies the perception or knowledge of it. Disobedience to moral law, then, implies the development in the reason of the idea of the good or valuable to being. A being therefore who does not possess reason, or the ideas of whose reason on moral subjects are not at all developed, cannot violate the law of God; for over such the moral law does not extend its claims.

3. Disobedience to moral law implies the development of the idea of the good or the valuable, that is, the idea of moral obligation to will or choose it for the sake of its intrinsic value. When the value of being is once developed, the mind cannot but instantly or simultaneously affirm its obligation to will it as an end and every good according to its perceived relative value.

4. Disobedience to moral law implies the development of the idea of moral obligation, namely, the idea of right and wrong: that it is right to will good and wrong not to will it, or to will it only partially. This idea is the correlative of the idea of moral obligation, and the development of the former necessitates the development of the latter.

5. Disobedience to moral law also implies the development of the ideas of right and wrong—namely, the idea of praise or blameworthiness, or of virtue and vice, or, in other words, of *guilt* and innocence. The idea of moral character is the correlative of that of right and wrong in such a sense that the idea of right and wrong necessitates and implies the idea of moral character or of praise and blameworthiness. When these conditions are fulfilled, and not till then, the spirit of self-seeking, or the choice of our own gratification as an end, becomes sin or constitutes a breach of moral law. It will follow that no beings are subjects of moral government and capable of disobedience to moral law but such as are moral agents. That means that only beings that possess both the powers of moral agency and have these powers in such a state of development and integrity as to render obedience possible can be considered moral agents. Accordingly, neither brute animals, nor idiots, nor lunatics, nor somnambulists, nor indeed any being who is not *rational* and free can disobey the moral law.

We will now proceed to the immensely interesting and important task of contrasting benevolence with selfishness in the meditations that follow.

1

LOVE IS VOLITIONAL

"And now these three remain: faith, hope and love. But the greatest of these is love" (1 Cor. 13:13).

As I proceed to discuss the attributes of love, I will call attention to the states of the intellect and of the emotions, and also to the courses of outward conduct implied in the existence of this love in any mind. Certain states of the intellect, along with various emotions and outward actions, necessarily result from this love by the law of cause and effect.

Love is a phenomenon of the will. Love is *volitional*. There is a state of the emotions often expressed by the term *love*. Love may and often does exist, as everyone knows, in the form of a mere feeling or emotion. The term is often used to express the emotion of fondness or attachment as distinct from a volitional state of mind or a choice of the will. This emotion or feeling, as we are all aware, is purely an involuntary state of mind. Because it is a phenomenon of the sensibility, and of course a passive state of mind, it has in itself no moral character. The law of God requires volitional love or good will. This love consists in choice or intention. It is choosing the highest well-being of God and the universe of conscious or rational beings as an ultimate purpose. Of course volition must be one of love's characteristics.

If love is volitional, or consists in choice, if love is a phenomenon of the will, it must control the thoughts of the mind and the states of the emotions as well as the outward actions. This love, then, not only consists in a state of consecration to God and the universe, but also implies deep emotions of love to God and others. Though it is a phenomenon of the will, it implies the existence of all those feelings of love and affection to God and others that necessarily result from the consecration of the heart or will to their highest well-being. This love also implies all that outward course of life that necessarily flows from a state of will consecrated to this end. Let it be borne in mind that when these feelings do not arise in the sensibility, and when this course of life is not present, then the true love or the voluntary consecration to God and the universe required by the law of God is not present. These states of feeling and outward actions must flow from this love by a law of necessity. These feelings or emotions of love and a correct outward life may exist without this volitional love, as I shall point out later; but this love cannot exist without those feelings and appropriate actions, since they flow from it by a law of necessity. These emotions will vary in their strength as constitution and circumstances vary in different people, but they must exist in some noticeable degree whenever the will is in a benevolent attitude.

Liberty is an attribute of love. The mind is free and spontaneous in its exercise. The will has liberty when it has the power at every moment to choose self-gratification instead of love as an end. Of this fact every moral agent is conscious. Love, therefore, is a free and responsible choice.

Selfishness has often been confused with mere desire. But selfishness, too, is volitional. Selfishness and desire are by no means identical. Desire is natural: we were made to have desires. Desire is a phenomenon of the sensibility. Desire is a purely involuntary state of mind, and can in itself produce no action, and can have no moral character of itself.

Clearly, then, selfishness is a phenomenon of the will, and consists in committing the will to the gratification of the desires. The desire itself is not selfishness, but submitting the will to be governed by the desires is selfishness. It should be understood that no kind of mere desire, and no strength of mere desire constitutes selfishness. Selfishness begins when the will yields to the desire and seeks to obey it in opposition to the law of the intelligence or the law of God. It matters not what kind of desire it is; if it is the desire that governs the will, this is selfishness. Selfishness, then, exists when the will has been given over to the gratification of desire.

Liberty is an attribute of selfishness as well as of love. This means that the choice of self-gratification is not necessitated by desire. But the will is always free to choose in opposition to desire. Every moral agent is as conscious of this fact as he is of his own existence. The desire is not free, but the choice to gratify it is and must be free. There is a sense in which slavery is an attribute of selfishness, but not in the sense that the will chooses to gratify desire by a law of necessity. Slavery to selfishness develops over a period of time as the will is habitually committed to self-gratification. Liberty, in the sense of the ability to make an opposite choice, must ever remain an attribute of selfishness, while selfishness continues to be a sin, or while it continues to sustain any relation to moral law.

Each person must choose whether he will love God and his fellow human beings or live selfishly to gratify himself.

FOR REFLECTION

I have decided to consecrate myself to loving God and others, rather than allow my feelings and actions to flow from a decision to gratify my selfish desires.

2

LOVE IS INTELLIGENT

"If I have the gift of prophecy and can fathom all mysteries and all knowledge, and if I have a faith that can move mountains, but have not love, I am nothing" (1 Cor. 13:2).

When I say love is intelligent, I mean that the mind chooses love as an end *intelligently*. We know what we choose, why we choose it, and that we do so in accordance with the direction of our intelligence. We know whether or not an end is worthy of being chosen. Because of its value, intelligence demands what should be chosen. The mind knows that because of its own intrinsic value love should be chosen.

Volition, liberty, and intelligence are *natural attributes of love*; therefore, the other meditations discuss the *moral attributes of love*. We could not love without these natural attributes, and we could not be guilty of being selfish without these natural attributes as a vital part of our being.

When we say that intelligence is also an attribute of selfishness, we do not intend that intelligence is an attribute or phenomenon of will, or that the choice of self-gratification is in accordance with the demands of the intelligence. But I intend to say that the choice is made with the knowledge of the moral character involved in it. The mind knows its obligation to make an opposite choice from the choice of self-gratification. It is not a mistake. It is not a choice made in ignorance of moral obligation to choose the highest good of being as an end in opposition to self-gratification. It is an intelligent choice in the sense that *it is a known resistance of the demands of the intelligence.* It is a conscious rejection of the claims of intelligence, a conscious setting up of self-gratification as the end chosen, and a preferring of it to all higher interests.

Selfishness is *unreasonable,* while love is reasonable. Selfish choice is in direct opposition to the demands of reason. The reason was given to rule by the imposition of law and moral obligation. Obedience to moral law as it is revealed in the reason is virtue, but obedience to feelings in opposition to the reason is sin.

Selfishness consists in dethroning reason from the seat of government and enthroning blind desire in opposition to it. Selfishness is always and by necessity unreasonable. It is a denial of that divine attribute that allies human beings to God and makes us capable of virtue. Selfishness dethrones reason and sinks human beings to the level of a brute. It is a denial of his humanness and his rational nature. It is a contempt for the voice of God within him, and a deliberate trampling down of the sovereignty of his own intelligence. Shame on selfishness! It dethrones human reason, would dethrone the Divine mind, and would place blind lust upon the throne of the universe.

The very definition of selfishness in opposition to true love implies that unreasonableness is one of its attributes. Selfishness is the will's yielding itself to the impulses of the sensibility in opposition to the demands of the intelligence. Therefore, every act or choice of the will is necessarily either reasonable or altogether unreasonable. The sinner, while he continues as such, never says or does one thing that is in accordance with right reason. Hence the Bible says that "madness is in their heart while they live" (Eccls. 9:3). They have made an unreasonable choice for their supreme intention, and all their choices of means to secure their end are only a carrying out of that ultimate choice. The means they choose are a deliberate attempt to secure an end contrary to reason. Therefore, no sinner who has never been converted, has, even in a single instance, chosen otherwise than in direct opposition to reason.

Sinners are not merely sometimes unreasonable, but *con-*

sistently; and while they remain selfish, *necessarily so*. The very first time that a sinner acts or wills reasonably is when he turns to God, or repents and becomes a Christian. This is the first instance in which he, in effect, acknowledges that he has reason. Previous to this, virtually every one of the actions of his will and of his life is a denial of his humanness, of his rational nature, and of his obligation to God and to his neighbor.

We sometimes hear impenitent sinners spoken of as being unreasonable, and in such a manner as to imply that all sinners are not so. But this only favors their delusion that supposes they are not all at all times altogether unreasonable. But the fact is, there is not, and there never can be in earth or hell, one impenitent sinner who in any instance acts otherwise than in direct and concrete opposition to his reason.

It would, therefore, have been infinitely better for sinners if they had never been endowed with reason. They do not merely act without consulting their reason, but in bold and determined opposition to it.

Sinners act as directly in opposition to their reason as they possibly can. They not only oppose reason, but they oppose it as much and in as aggravated a manner as possible. What can be more directly and aggravatedly opposed to reason than the choice of selfish gratification which the sinner makes as his end or ultimate goal? The ability to reason was given him to direct him with regard to the supreme choice of his life. Reason imparts to him the idea of the eternal and the infinite. It sets before him the interests of God and of the universe as having absolutely infinite value. It affirms their value and the infinite obligation of the sinner to consecrate himself to these interests, and it promises him endless rewards if he will do so.

Reason also lays before him the consequences of his refusal. It thunders in his ear the terrible sanctions of the law. It points him to the coming doom that awaits his refusal to comply with its demands. But in the face of all this evidence and these affirmations of reason with its demands and threatenings, the sinner unhesitatingly turns away and consecrates himself to the gratification of his own selfish desires. He does it with the certainty that he could not do greater harm to his own nature than in this most mad, most preposterous, most blasphemous choice. Sinners should consider that it is impossible for them to offer a greater insult to God, who gave them reason, or to more truly and deeply shame and degrade themselves, when they continue in their beastly selfishness.

Total, universal, and shameless unreasonableness is the universal characteristic of every selfish mind. True love for God and others is the most reasonable state for the Christian to maintain.

FOR REFLECTION

Doing God's will is my ultimate goal; therefore, my choices and actions are more reasonable and intelligent. I do not live in delusion and meaninglessness, because I refuse to live primarily to gratify myself.

3

LOVE IS DISINTERESTED

"Love is patient, love is kind. It does not envy, it does not boast, it is not proud. It is not rude, it is not self-seeking, it is not easily angered, it keeps no record of wrongs" (1 Cor. 13:4, 5).

Disinterestedness is another attribute of this love. By disinterestedness I do not mean that the mind takes no interest in the object loved, but rather the opposite. It takes a supreme interest in it. But the term disinterested expresses the mind's choice of an end for its own sake, and not merely on condition that the good belongs to self. This love is disinterested in the sense that the highest well-being of God and the universe is chosen, not on condition of its relation to self, but for its own intrinsic and infinite value. It is this attribute, particularly, that distinguishes this love from selfish love. Selfish love makes the relation of good to self the condition for choosing it. The good of God and the universe, if chosen at all, is only chosen as a means or condition of promoting the highest good of self. But this love does not make good to self its end. It chooses good to God and being in general as its chief end.

Since disinterestedness is an attribute of this love, it does not seek its own good but that of others. "Love is not self-seeking." Love grasps the good of being in general, and as a natural result produces a corresponding outward life and inward feeling. The intelligence will be employed in devising ways and means for the promotion of its end. The sensibility will be very much alive to the good of everyone. It will rejoice in the good of others as well as its own, and will grieve at the misery of others as well as its own. It "will rejoice with them who do rejoice, and weep with them that weep." There will not, cannot be envy at the prosperity of others, but unfeigned joy, joy as real and often as exquisite as in its own.

Benevolence enjoys everyone's good things, while selfishness is too envious at the good things of others to even enjoy its own. There is a divine economy in benevolence. Each benevolent soul enjoys not only his own good things, but also the good things of all others, rejoicing in their happiness. He drinks at the river of God's pleasure. He rejoices not only in doing good to others, but also in observing their enjoyment of good things. He joys in God's joy and in the joy of angels and saints. He also rejoices in the good things of all conscious beings. He is happy in watching the pleasure of the beasts of the field, the fowls of the air, and the fish of the sea. He sympathizes with all joy and all suffering known to him. Nor is his sympathy with the suffering of others a feeling of unmingled pain. It is a real privilege to sympathize in the woes of others. He would not be without this sympathy. It agrees with his sense of propriety and fitness, that mingled with the painful emotion there is a sweet feeling of self-approbation, so that a benevolent sympathy with the woes of others is by no means inconsistent with happiness, and with perfect happiness.

God has this sympathy. He often expresses and manifests it. There is indeed a mysterious and an exquisite luxury in sharing the woes of others. God and the angels and all holy beings know what it is. Where this result of love is not manifested, love itself is absent. Envy at the prosperity, influence, or good of others, the absence of sensible joy in view of the good enjoyed by others, and of sympathy with the sufferings of others, prove conclusively that this love does not exist. There is an expansiveness, an ampleness of embrace, a universality and a divine disinterestedness in this love that necessarily manifests itself in the generous devising of great things for Zion. It is also shown in the rich outpourings of the floods of sympathetic feeling, both of joys and sorrows, as their occasions present themselves before the mind.

Interestedness is an attribute of selfishness, by this I mean *self*-interestedness. It is not the disinterested choice of good; that is, it is not the choice of the good of being in general as an end, but it is the choice of self-good, of good to self. It is chosen solely because it benefits self. Except for its being the good of self it would not be chosen. The intrinsic value of good, which is the fundamental reason that should induce choice, is rejected as insufficient. Instead, the secondary reason, namely, its relation or benefit to self, is the condition which determines the will. This is really making self-good the end. In other words, it is making *self-gratification* the supreme end. Virtually, nothing is regarded as worthy of choice except that which will satisfy one's self-gratification.

This attribute of selfishness produces a corresponding state in the emotions. The feelings under such indulgence achieve a monstrous development, sometimes generally, but more frequently in some particular directions. Selfishness is the committal of the will to the indulgence of the propensities, strong longings, appetites, or tendencies. But from this it by no means follows that all of the tendencies will be indiscriminately indulged and thereby greatly developed. Sometimes one appetite and sometimes another has the greatest natural strength, and thereby gains the ascendancy in the control of the will. Sometimes circumstances tend to develop one appetite or passion more strongly than another. Whatever desire is indulged the most will gain the greatest development.

The propensities cannot all be indulged at once, for they are often opposed to each other. But they may all be indulged and developed in their turn. For example, the licentious tendencies, the inclinations to various indulgences, cannot be indulged consistently with the simultaneous indulgence of the avaricious tendencies, the desire for reputation and for ultimate happiness. These tendencies, as well as the rest, may press in for gratification and in some instances may gain so equal a share of indulgence to be about equally developed. But in general, either from natural temperament, or from circumstances, one or more of the appetites will gain so uniform a control of the will as to give rise to its monstrous development. It may be the love of reputation. In that case, there will at least be a decent public behavior, more or less strict according to the state of morals in the society in which the individual lives. If it is love of sensual pleasure that gains the ascendancy over the other appetites, licentiousness will be the result. If it is love of food, then gluttony and epicurianism will be the result. The result of selfishness must be to develop in general, or in particular, the tendencies of the sensibility, emotionally or physically, and to produce a corresponding outward behavior.

If avarice takes control of the will, we have the tired, ragged miser. All the other propensities wither under the reign of this detestable one.

Where the love of knowledge prevails, we have the scholar, the philosopher, the man of learning. This disguises itself as one of the most decent and respectable forms of selfishness, but is nevertheless as absolutely selfish as any other form.

When compassion as a feeling prevails, we have as a result the philanthropist and often the reformer; not the reformer in a virtuous sense, but the selfish reformer.

Where love of kindred prevails, we often have the kind husband, the affectionate father, mother, brother, sister, and so on. These are the amiable sinners, especially among their own kindred.

When the love of country prevails, we have the patriot, the statesman, and the soldier. This picture may be drawn at full length, but with these traits I must leave you to fill up the outline. I would only add that several of these forms of selfishness so nearly resemble certain forms of virtue that they often are confused with them and mistaken for them.

FOR REFLECTION

I maintain the virtues that I have out of supreme love for God and not out of a selfish love for reputation.

4

LOVE IS IMPARTIAL

"But I tell you: Love your enemies and pray for those who persecute you, that you may be sons of your Father in heaven. He causes his sun to rise on the evil and the good, and sends rain on the righteous and the unrighteous" (Matt. 5:44–45).

Impartiality is another attribute of this love. By this term I do not mean that the mind is indifferent to the character of him who is happy or miserable; that it would be as well pleased to see the wicked as the righteous eternally and perfectly blessed. But it is intended that, other things being equal, it is the intrinsic value of their well-being which alone is regarded by the mind. In spite of these things, it matters not to whom the good belongs. Love is no respecter of persons. The purpose of love is the good of being, and it seeks to promote every interest according to its relative value.

Selfish love is partial. Selfish love seeks to promote self-interest first, and secondly those interests that in some way will at least indirectly promote the gratification of self. Selfish love has its favorites, its prejudices; it is unreasonable and ridiculous. Color, family, nation, and many other things of a similar nature modify selfish love. But benevolence knows neither Jew nor Greek, neither bond nor free, white nor black, Barbarian, Cythian, European, Asiatic, African, nor American. It esteems all men as men, and by virtue of their common manhood calls every man a brother, and seeks the best interest of all.

Impartiality, as an attribute of benevolence, will of course manifest itself in the outward life and in the temperament and spirit of its subject. This love can have no fellowship with those absurd and ridiculous prejudices that are so often prevalent among nominal Christians. Nor will it cherish them for a moment in the sensuality of him who exercises it. Benevolence recognizes neither privileged classes nor excluded classes. Benevolence produces in the feelings an utter loathing of those discriminations so odiously manifested and boasted of which are founded exclusively in a selfish state of the will. The fact that a man is a man (and not that he is of our party, of our race, or of our town, state or nation), that he is a creature of God, that he is capable of virtue and happiness—these are the principal considerations this divinely impartial love focuses on. It is the intrinsic value of his interests, and not that they are the interests of one connected with self that the benevolent mind regards.

But here it is important to remark that the economy of benevolence demands that where two interests are in themselves considered of equal value, in order to ensure the greatest amount of good, each one should concentrate his efforts where they can be used to the greatest advantage. For example, every person has relationships in which he can accomplish more good by seeking to promote the interest and happiness of certain persons rather than others. His family, his relatives, his companions, his immediate neighbors and those to whom in the providence of God he has a relationship give him access to and influence over them. Therefore, while benevolence regards every interest according to its relative value, it reasonably exercises its efforts in the direction where there is the prospect of accomplishing the most good.

This, I say, is not partiality, but impartiality; for it is not the particular persons to whom good can be done, but the amount of good that can be accomplished that directs the efforts of benevolence. It is not because my family is my own, nor because their well-being is, of course, more valuable in itself than that of my neighbors' families, but because my relationships with them afford me higher facilities for doing them good, I am under particular obligation to aim first at promoting their good. Hence the Apostle says, "If any man provide not for his own, especially for those of his own household, he hath denied the faith and is worse than an infidel" (1 Tim. 5:8).

Strictly speaking, benevolence esteems every known good according to its intrinsic and relative value; but practically treats every interest according to the perceived probability of securing on the whole the highest amount of good. This is a truth of great practical importance. It is developed in the experience and observation of every day and hour. We see it manifested in the conduct of God and of Christ, of apostles and of martyrs. It is everywhere assumed in the precepts of the Bible, and manifested throughout the history of benevolent effort. Let it be understood, then, that impartiality, as an attribute of benevolence, does not imply that its effort to do good will not be modified by relationships and circumstances. But, on the contrary, this attribute implies that the efforts to secure the great end of benevolence—that is, the greatest good to God and the universe—will be modified by those relationships and circumstances that afford the highest advantages for doing good.

The impartiality of benevolence always causes it to lay supreme stress upon God's interests, because His well-being is of infinite value, and of course benevolence must be supreme to Him. Benevolence being impartial love, of course, perceives God's interests and well-being as of infinitely greater value than the sum total of all other interests. Benevolence regards our neighbor's interests as our own simply because they are, in their intrinsic value, as our own. Benevolence, therefore, is always supreme to God and equal to man.

Conversely, *partiality* is an attribute of selfishness. Partiality consists in preferring certain interests because they are either directly the interests of self, or so connected with self-interest as to be preferred for that reason. It does not matter whether the preference centers on an interest of greater or lesser value if it is preferred not for the reason of its greater value, but because of its advantage to self. In some instances the *practical* preference may justly be given to an interest of lesser value because we are in a closer relationship which facilitates securing it, when the greater interest could not be secured by us. If the reason for the preference in such a case is not that it is *self-interest*, but an interest that can be secured while the greater cannot, the preference is a just one, not partiality.

My family, for example, has such a relation to me that I can more readily and surely secure their interests than those of my neighbor or of a stranger. For this reason I am under obligation to give the practical preference to the interests of my own family, not because they are my own, but because I can more readily secure their interests, although they may be of no greater, or even of less intrinsic value, than the interests of many other families.

The question here centers on the amount I am *able to secure*, and not merely on their intrinsic value. It is a general truth that we can secure more readily and certainly the interests of those to whom we have closer relationships; therefore, God and reason point out these interests as particular objects of our attention and effort. This is not partiality but impartiality. It is treating interests as they should be treated.

Selfishness, however, is always partial. If it gives any interest the preference, it is because of its relationship to self. It always, because of its nature, *necessarily* places the greatest stress upon and gives preference to those interests which will promote *self-gratification*.

Here care should be taken to avoid delusion. Oftentimes selfishness appears to be very disinterested and impartial. For example, take a person whose compassion, as a mere feeling or state of the sensibility, is greatly developed. He meets a beggar, an object that strongly excites his ruling passion. He empties his pockets, and even takes off his coat and gives it to him, and in his excitement he will divide all he has with him or even give him all. Now for most, this would generally pass for undoubted virtue, as a rare and impressive instance of moral goodness. But there is no virtue, no benevolence in it. It is the mere yielding of the will to the control of feeling and has nothing in it of the nature of virtue. Innumerable examples of this might be cited as illustrations of this truth. It is only an instance and an illustration of selfishness. It is the will seeking to gratify the feeling of compassion.

We naturally desire not only our own happiness, but also that of people in general when their happiness in no way conflicts with our own. Hence, selfish people will often manifest a deep interest in the welfare of those whose welfare will not interfere with their own. Now, if the will in some instance is yielded up to the gratification of this desire, this would often be regarded as virtue. For example, a few years ago much interest and feeling was excited in this country by the cause and sufferings of the Greeks in their struggle for liberty. A spirit of enthusiasm appeared, and many were ready to give and do almost anything for the cause of liberty. They gave up their will to the gratification of this excited state of feeling. This, they may have supposed, was virtue; but it was not, nor was there a semblance of virtue about it. This becomes clear when it is understood that virtue consists in yielding the will to the law of the intelligence, not to the impulse of excited feelings.

Some writers have fallen into the strange mistake of making virtue equivalent to seeking the gratification of *certain* desires, because, as they say, these desires are virtuous. They make some of the desires selfish and some benevolent. To yield the will to the control of the selfish tendencies is sin. To yield the will to the control of the benevolent desires, such as the desire of my neighbor's happiness and public happiness, is virtue, because these are *good* desires while the selfish desires are *evil*. This ascribing of certain desires as virtuous is and has been a very common view of virtue and vice, but it is fundamentally erroneous. None of the natural desires are good or evil in themselves. They are all involuntary and all terminate on their respective objects. To yield the will to the control of any one of them, no matter which, is sin. It is following a blind feeling, desire or impulse of the sensibility instead of yielding to the demands of the intelligence. To will the good of my neighbor or of my country and of God because of the intrinsic value of those interests—that is, to will them as an end and in obedience to the law of the reason—is virtue; but to will them to gratify a natural but blind desire is selfishness and sin. The desires, to be sure, terminate on their respective objects, but the will in this case seeks the objects, not for their own sake, but because they are desired. That is to gratify the desires. This is choosing them not as an end but as a means of self-gratification, and making self-gratification the end after all. This must be a universal truth when a thing is chosen in obedience to desire. The benevolence of these writers is sheer selfishness, and their virtue is vice.

The choice of anything because it is desired is selfishness and sin. It matters not what it is. The very statement that I choose a thing because I desire it is only another form of saying that I choose it for my own sake, or for the sake of appeasing the desire, and not on account of its own intrinsic value. All such choice is always and necessarily partial. It is giving one interest the preference over another, not because of its perceived intrinsic and superior value, but because it is an object of desire. If I yield to desire in any case, it must be to gratify the desire. This is and, in the case supposed, must be the end for which the choice is made. To deny this is to deny that the will seeks the object because it is desired. Partiality consists in giving one thing the preference of another for no good reason— that is, not because the intelligence demands this preference, but because emotions demand it. Partiality is therefore always and necessarily an attribute of selfishness.

FOR REFLECTION

I have good and sufficient reasons for fulfilling my desires; such as the desire to show compassion or be healthy, I do not simply follow my desires wherever they lead me.

5

LOVE IS UNIVERSAL

"If you love those who love you, what reward will you get? Are not even the tax collectors doing that? And if you greet only your brothers, what are you doing more than others? Do not even pagans do that? Be perfect, therefore, as your heavenly Father is perfect" (Matt. 5:46–48).

Another attribute of this love is *universality*. Benevolence chooses the highest good of being in general. It excludes none from its regard; but on the contrary embraces all. But by this it is not intended that it seeks to promote the good of every individual. It seeks the highest practicable amount of good. The interest of every individual is estimated according to its intrinsic value, whatever the circumstances or character of each may be. Character and relationships may and must modify the manifestations of benevolence, or its efforts in seeking to promote this end.

A wicked character and governmental relations and considerations may forbid benevolence to seek the good of some. In fact, they may demand that positive misery shall be inflicted on some as a warning to others to beware of their destructive ways. Universality, as an attribute of benevolence, intends that goodwill be truly exercised toward all conscious beings whatever their character and relations may be. It also means that when the higher good of the greater number does not forbid it, the happiness of all and of each will be pursued with an effort equal to their relative value and the prospect of securing each interest. Enemies as well as friends, strangers and foreigners as well as relations and immediate neighbors will be enfolded in its sweet embrace. It is the state of mind required by Christ in the divine precept, "I say unto you, love your enemies, pray for them that hate you, and do good unto them that despitefully use and persecute you" (Matt. 5:44). This attribute of benevolence is gloriously conspicuous in the character of God. His love to sinners alone accounts for our being out of hell today. His intention to secure the highest good of the greatest number is illustrated by the display of His glorious justice in the punishment of the wicked. His universal care for all ranks and conditions of conscious beings manifested in His works and providence, beautifully and gloriously illustrates the truth that "his tender mercies are over all his works" (Ps. 145:9).

It is easy to see that universality must be a modification of true benevolence. It consists in good willing—that is, in choosing the highest good of being as such and for its own sake. Of course, it must, to be consistent with itself, seek the good of all and of each, so far as the good of each is consistent with the greatest good upon the whole. Benevolence not only wills and seeks the good of moral beings, but also the good of every conscious existence, from the minutest animal to the highest order of beings. It of course begets a state of the emotions that is vibrantly alive to all happiness and all pain. It will be pained with the agony of an insect, and also rejoice in its joy. God does this and all holy beings do this. Where this sympathy with the joys and sorrows of universal being is absent, there is no benevolence. Observe, good is its final intention. Where this end is promoted by the proper means, the feelings are gratified. Where evil is witnessed, the benevolent spirit deeply and necessarily sympathizes.

Efficiency is another attribute or characteristic of benevolence. Benevolence consists in choice or intention. Now, we know from consciousness that choice or intention constitutes the mind's deepest activity. If I honestly intend a thing, I can make efforts to accomplish that which I intend, provided that I believe the thing possible. If I choose an end, this choice must and will energize to secure its end. When benevolence is the supreme choice—preference, intention of the soul—it is plainly impossible that it should not produce efforts to secure its end. It must, however, cease to exist or manifest itself in exertions to secure its end as soon as and whenever the intelligence deems it wise to do so. If the will has yielded to the intelligence in the choice of an end, it will certainly obey the intelligence in pursuit of that end. Choice, or intention, is the cause of all outward activity of moral agents. They all have chosen some end, either their own gratification or the highest good of being; and all the busy bustle of this world's teeming population is nothing else than choice or intention seeking to obtain its end.

Efficiency, therefore, is an attribute of benevolent intention. It must, it will, it does energize in God, in angels, in saints on earth and in heaven. It was this attribute of benevolence that led God to give His only begotten Son, and that led the Son to give himself "that whosoever believeth in him should not perish but have everlasting life" (John 3:16).

If love is efficient to produce outward action and inward feelings, it is efficient to wake up the intellect and set the world of thought on fire in devising ways and means to realize its end. It wields all the infinite natural attributes of God. It is the mainspring that moves all heaven, the mighty power that is heaving the mass of mind and rocking the moral world like a smothered volcano. Look to the heavens above. It was benevolence that hung them out. It is benevolence that sustains those mighty rolling orbs in their courses. It was goodwill endeavoring to realize its end that at first put forth creative power. That same power for the same reason still energizes and will continue to energize for the realization of its end so long as God is benevolent. And what a glorious thought that infinite benevolence is wielding and will forever wield infinite attributes for the promotion of good. No mind but an infinite mind can begin to conceive of the amount of good that God will secure. Oh, blessed glorious thoughts! But it is, it must be a reality as surely as God and the universe exist. It is no imagination; it is one of the most stable as well as the most glorious truths in the universe. Mountains of granite are but vapor in comparison with it. But will the truly benevolent on earth and in heaven sympathize with God? The power that energizes Him energizes them. One principle animates and moves them all, and that principle is love—goodwill to universal being. Our souls may well cry out, "Amen, go on, God-speed; let the mighty power heave and wield universal mind until all the ills of earth shall be put away and until all that can be made holy are clothed in the garments of everlasting gladness!"

Since benevolence is necessarily, from its very nature, active and efficient in putting forth efforts to secure its end, and since its end is the highest good of being, it follows that all who are truly religious will and must, from the very nature of true religion, be active in endeavoring to promote the good of being. While effort is possible to a Christian, it is as natural to him as breathing. He has within him the very mainspring of activity, a heart set on the promotion of the highest good of universal being. This is the end for which he lives and moves and has his being. While he has life and activity at all, it will, and it must be directed to this end. Let this never be forgotten. An idle, inactive, inefficient Christian is a misnomer. Religion is essentially an active principle, and when and while it exists, it must exercise and manifest itself. It is not merely good desire, but it is good willing. Men may have desires, and hope and live on them, without making efforts to realize their desires. They may desire without action. If their will is active, their life must be. If they really choose an ultimate end, this choice must manifest itself. The sinner does and must manifest his selfish choice, and so likewise must the saint manifest his benevolence.

Selfishness is also efficient. *Desire* never produces action until it influences the will. It has no efficiency or causality in itself. It cannot without the concurrence of the will, command the attention of the intellect, or move a muscle of the body. The whole causality of the mind resides in the will. In it lies the power of accomplishment.

The whole efficiency of the mind in regard to accomplishment resides in the choice of an end or in the ultimate intention. All action of the will or all willing must consist in choosing either an end or the means of accomplishing an end. If there is choice, something is chosen. That something is chosen for some reason. To deny this is a denial that anything is chosen. The reason for the choice and the thing chosen are identical. This we have repeatedly seen.

The means to an end cannot be chosen until the end is chosen. The choice of the end is distinct from the volitions or endeavors of the mind to secure the end. But although the choice of an end is not identical with the subordinate choices and volitions to attain the end, it still necessitates them. The choice once made, secures or necessitates the executive volitions to attain the end. By this I do not mean that the mind is not free to relinquish its end, and of course to relinquish the use of the means to accomplish it; but only that, while the choice or intention remains, the choice of the end is efficient in producing efforts to realize the end. This is true both of benevolence and selfishness. They are both choices of an end, and are necessarily efficient in producing the use of the means to realize this end. They are choices of opposite ends, and of course will produce their respective results.

The Bible represents sinners as having eyes full of adultery and that cannot cease from sin; that while the will is committed to the indulgence of the propensities, they cannot cease from the indulgence. There is no way, therefore, for the sinner to escape from committing sin, except to cease to be selfish. As long as selfishness continues, you may change its form of outward manifestation, you may deny one appetite or desire for the sake of indulging another; but it is and still must be sin. The desire to escape hell and to obtain heaven may become the strongest, in which case selfishness will take on a most sanctimonious air. But if the will is following desire, it is still selfishness; and all your religious duties, as you call them, are only selfishness robed in the stolen garments of love.

Remember then that selfishness is choice. Selfishness is the ultimate intention. It is and must be efficient in producing its effects. It is cause; the effect must follow. The whole life and activity of sinners is founded in it. It constitutes their life, or rather their spiritual death. They are dead in trespasses and in sins. It is in vain for them to dream of doing anything good until they relinquish their selfishness. While this continues, they cannot act at all except as they use the means to accomplish a selfish end. It is impossible while the will remains committed to a selfish end or to the promotion of self-interest or self-gratification that it should use the means to promote a benevolent end. The first thing is to change the end, and then the sinner can cease from outward sin. Indeed, if the end is changed, the same acts which were sinful before will now become holy. While the selfish end continued, whatever the sinner did was totally selfish. Whether he ate, drank, labored, or preached; whatever he did was to promote some form of self-interest. The end being wrong, all was and must have been wrong.

But let that selfish end be changed. Let benevolence take the place of selfishness, and all will become right. With this end in view, the mind is absolutely incapable of doing or choosing anything except as a means of promoting the good of the universe.

FOR REFLECTION

As I examine the way I spend most of my time and energy, I know I am not indulging selfish goals but living for benevolent purposes.

6

LOVE IS PENITENT

"Or do you show contempt for the riches of his kindness, tolerance and patience, not realizing that God's kindness leads you toward repentance" (Rom. 2:4).

I wish to impress this truth deeply upon your mind. Let me summarize some preceding remarks in the form of definite propositions.

1. All action consists in or results from choice.

2. All choice must refer to or consist in the choice of an end or of means. The mind is incapable of choosing unless it has an object of choice, and that object must be regarded by the mind either as an end or as a means.

3. The mind can have but one ultimate end at the same time.

4. The mind cannot choose the means until it has chosen the end.

5. The mind cannot choose one end and use means to accomplish another at the same time.

6. Therefore, while the will is benevolent or committed to the glory of God and the good of being, it cannot use the means of self-gratification, or exercise selfish volitions.

7. When the will is committed to self-indulgence, it cannot use the means designed to glorify God and promote the good of people as an end. This is impossible.

8. The carnal heart or mind can only sin; it is not subject to

the law of God, neither indeed can be, because it is "enmity against God."

9. The new or regenerate heart cannot continue in willful sin. It is benevolence, love to God and man. This cannot sin. These are both ultimate choices or intentions. They are by their own nature each efficient in excluding the other, and each in securing for the time being the exclusive use of means to promote its own end. To deny this is the same absurdity as to maintain either that the will can at the same time choose two opposite ends, or that it can choose one end only, but at the same time choose the means to accomplish another end not yet chosen. Now, either alternative is absurd. Holiness and sin, therefore, can never coexist in the same mind. As has been said, for the time being, each necessarily excludes the other. Selfishness and benevolence coexist in the same mind? Never! A greater absurdity and a more gross contradiction was never conceived or expressed.

No one for a moment ever supposed that selfishness and benevolence could coexist in the same mind; if he had clearly defined ideas of what they are. When *desire*, on the one hand, is mistaken for benevolence, and on the other, for selfishness, the mistake is natural that selfishness and benevolence can coexist in the same mind. But as soon as it is seen that benevolence and selfishness are supreme ultimate opposite choices, the affirmation is instantaneous and irresistible that they can neither coexist, nor can one use means to promote the other. While benevolence remains, the mind's whole activity springs from it as from a fountain.

This is the philosophy of Christ:

"Either make the tree good, and his fruit good; or else make the tree corrupt, and his fruit corrupt: for the tree is known by his fruit. A good man out of the good treasure of the heart bringeth forth good things: and an evil man out of the evil treasure bringeth forth evil things" (Matt. 12:33, 35).

"Doth a fountain send forth at the same place *sweet* water and *bitter?* Can the fig tree, my brethren, bear olive berries? either a vine figs? so *can* no fountain both yield salt water and fresh" (James 3:11, 12).

"For a good tree bringeth not forth corrupt fruit; neither doth a corrupt tree bring forth good fruit. For every tree is known by his own fruit: for of thorns men do not gather figs, nor of a bramble bush gather they grapes. A good man out of the good treasure of his heart bringeth forth that which is good; and an evil man out of the evil treasure of his heart, bringeth forth that which is evil; for out of the abundance of the heart his mouth speaketh" (Luke 6:43–45).

Penitence must be a characteristic of benevolence in one who has been a sinner. Penitence is not a phenomenon of the emotions, but of the will. Every form of virtue must, of necessity, be a phenomenon of the will, and not of the intellect or of the emotions. Penitence is also commonly used to designate a certain phenomenon of the feelings, that is, sorrow for sin. This sorrow, though called penitence, is not penitence regarded as a virtue. Evangelical penitence consists in a specific attitude of the will toward our own past sins. It is the will's continued rejection of and opposition to our past sins—the will's aversion to them. This rejection, opposition, and aversion is penitence, and is always a characteristic in the history of those benevolent minds that have been sinners. This change of will deeply and permanently affects the emotions. It will keep the intelligence thoroughly awake to the nature, character, and tendencies of sin, to its unspeakable guilt, and all its intrinsic odiousness. This will, of course, break up the fountains of the great deep of feeling. The emotions will often pour out a torrent of burning sorrow in view of past sin; and all its loathing and indignation will be kindled against it when it beholds it. This attribute of benevolence will produce confession and restitution, natural results from genuine repentance. If the soul forsakes sin, it will of course make all possible amends when it has committed an offense. Benevolence seeks the good of all and will and must seek to repair whatever injury it has inflicted on any.

Repentance will and must produce a God-justifying and self-condemning spirit. It will take all shame and all blame upon itself, and fully acquit God of all blame. This deep self-abasement is always and necessarily a characteristic of a truly penitent soul. Where this is absent, true repentance has not occurred.

I should, however, point out that feelings of self-loathing, of self-abasement, and of abhorrence of sin depend upon the view which the intelligence gains of the nature and guilt and aggravation of sin. In a sensible and manifested degree, it will always exist when the will has honestly turned or repented. This feeling I have described gains strength as the soul from time to time gains a deeper insight into the nature, guilt and tendencies of sin. It is probable that repentance as an emotion will always gain strength, not only in this world but in heaven. Can it be that the saints in heaven can reflect upon their past abuse of the Savior, and not feel their sorrow stirred within them? Nor will this diminish their happiness. Godly sorrow is not unhappiness. There is a luxury in the exercise. Remorse cannot be known in heaven, but godly sorrow, I think, must exist among the saints forever. However this may be in heaven, it certainly is implied in repentance on earth. This attribute must and will produce an outward life conformed to the law of love. There may be an outward morality without benevolence, but there cannot be benevolence without corresponding purity of outward life.

The opposite of this is *impenitence* which is another modification of selfishness. Perhaps it is more proper to say that impenitence is only another name for selfishness. Penitence or repentance is the turning of the heart from selfishness to benevolence. Impenitence is the heart's cleaving to the committing of sin, or more properly speaking, impenitence is cleaving to the willing and doing of that which is sin.

Enmity against God is an attribute of selfishness. Enmity is hatred. Hatred may exist either as a phenomenon of the emotions or as a state or attitude of the will. The hatred to which I refer now is the of enmity of heart or will. It is selfishness viewed in its relationships to God. That selfishness is enmity against God is evident from the following reasons:

1. The Bible condemns it. The Apostle Paul expressly says that "the carnal mind (minding the flesh) is enmity against God." It is fully evident that by the carnal mind the Apostle means obeying the tendencies or gratifying the desires. But this is selfishness as I have defined it.

2. Selfishness is directly opposed to the will of God as expressed in His law. His law requires benevolence. Selfishness is its opposite, and therefore enmity against the Lawgiver.

3. Selfishness is as hostile to God's government as it can be. It is directly opposed to every law and principle and measure of His moral government.

4. Selfishness is opposition to God's existence. Opposition to a government is opposition to the will of the governor. It is opposition to His *existence in that capacity or office*. It is and must be enmity against the existence of the ruler as such. Selfishness must be enmity against the existence of God's government, and as He does and must carry out the office of Sovereign Ruler, selfishness must be enmity against His life. Selfishness will tolerate no restraint in respect to attaining its end. There is nothing in the universe it will not sacrifice to self. This is true, or it is not selfishness. If God's happiness or government or life come into competition with it, they must be sacrificed.

5. God is the uncompromising enemy of selfishness. It is the abominable thing He hates. He stands more against the way of selfishness than all other moral beings. His opposition to selfishness is and must be supreme and perfect.

6. Selfishness is mortal enmity against God. God once took upon himself human nature and tried the experiment. Men could not tolerate His presence upon earth, and they did not rest until they had murdered Him.

7. Selfishness is supreme enmity against God. It is opposed to God more than to all other beings. This is necessarily so because God is totally opposed to selfishness and stands directly and eternally in its way. Selfishness must be relinquished or you place yourself in supreme opposition to God. Enmity against any body or thing besides God can be overcome more easily than against Him. All earthly enmities can be overcome by kindness and change of circumstances; but what kindness, what change of circumstances can change the human heart and overcome the selfishness and enmity that reigns there?

8. Selfishness offers all manner and every possible degree of resistance to God. It disregards God's commands. It views with contempt His authority. It spurns His mercy. It tramples

on His feelings. It tempts His forbearance. Selfishness in short is the universal antagonist and adversary of God. It can no more be reconciled to God or be subject to His law than it can cease to be selfishness.

There can be no benevolence in a human heart until there is repentance from selfishness and a turning from enmity toward God.

FOR REFLECTION

My sorrow for my past sin and enmity toward God motivates me to repudiate all selfishness and turn to Him in loving obedience in all things.

7

LOVE IS BELIEVING

"Love does not delight in evil but rejoices with the truth. It always protects, always trusts, always hopes, always perseveres" (1 Cor. 13:6, 7).

Faith is an attribute of benevolence. Evangelical faith is by no means, as some have supposed, a phenomenon of the intelligence. The term, however, is often used to express states of both the sensibility and the intellect. Conviction, or a strong perception of truth which eliminates doubt, is in common language called faith or belief, and this is done without any reference to the state of the will, whether it embraces or resists the truth perceived. Certainly, this conviction cannot be evangelical faith. In this belief, there is no virtue; it is the faith of devils. The term is often used in common speech to express a mere feeling of assurance, or confidence, and as often respects a falsehood as the truth. That is, people often feel the utmost confidence in a lie. Whether the feeling is in accordance with truth or falsehood, it is not faith in the evangelical sense of the term. It is not virtue.

Faith, to be a virtue, must be a phenomenon of the will. It must be an attribute of benevolence or love. As an attribute of benevolence, it is the will's embracing and loving truth. Faith is born when the soul yields or commits itself to the influence of truth. It is trust. It is when the heart embraces the truths of God's existence, attributes, works and Word. It implies intellectual perception of truth, and consists in the heart's embracing all the truth perceived.

It also implies that state of the sensibility which is called faith. Both the state of the intellect and the state of the sensibility just expressed are implied in faith, though neither of them make any part of it. Faith always produces a realizing state of the sensibility. The intellect sees the truth clearly, and the emotions feel it deeply, in proportion to the strength of the intellectual perception. It is possible, however, to have the clearest possible perception and the deepest possible felt assurance of the truth and yet be in a state of the utmost opposition of the will to the truth. This cannot be trust, confidence, faith. The damned in hell, no doubt, see the truth clearly, and have a feeling of the utmost assurance of the truth of Christianity, but they have no faith.

Faith, then, must certainly be a phenomenon of the will, and must be a modification or attribute of benevolence. It is goodwill, or benevolence, considered in its relationships to the truth of God. It is goodwill to God, confiding in His veracity and faithfulness, believing in Him. It cannot be overemphasized that every modification or phase of virtue is only benevolence existing in certain relationships, or goodwill to God and the universe manifesting itself in the various circumstances and relationships in which it is called to act.

Unbelief is a modification of selfishness. Unbelief is not a mere negation or the mere absence of faith. Faith is having confidence in God. Unbelief is the withholding of confidence in Him. Faith is a committal or yielding up of the will to be molded and influenced by truth. Unbelief is trusting in self and refusing to trust our souls and our interests to God's hands and to commit them to His disposal. Unbelief is saying, "I will take care of my own interests and let God take care of His. Who is God that I should serve Him, and what would it profit me to pray to Him?"

Unbelief is a refusal to commit ourselves to the guidance of God and a trusting in our own guidance. It is self-trust, self-dependence. And what is this but selfishness and self-seeking? Christ said to the Jews, "How can ye believe which seek honor one of another, and seek not the honor that cometh from God only?" (John 5:44). This assumes that unbelief is a modification of selfishness; that their regard for their reputation with men rendered faith impossible, while they indulged in that self-seeking spirit. They withheld confidence in Christ because to believe would cost them their reputation with men. So every sinner who ever heard the gospel and has not embraced it, withholds confidence in Christ because it will cost self too much to yield this confidence.

This is true in every case of unbelief. Confidence is withheld because to yield it involves and implies the denying of ourselves all ungodliness and every worldly lust. Christ demands the abandonment of every form and degree of selfishness. To believe is to receive with the heart Christ's instruction and requirements. To trust in them—to commit our whole being to be molded by them. Now, who does not see that unbelief is only a selfish withholding of this confidence, this committal? The fact is that faith implies and consists in yielding up selfishness and believing in God and His Word; unbelief is only selfishness contemplated or considered in its relations to Christ and His gospel.

FOR REFLECTION

I will be certain that there is no area of practical unbelief in my life, where I have not trusted something or a part of my life to the safe care and keeping of a true, loving and faithful God.

8

LOVE IS COMPLACENT

"But if anyone obeys his word, God's love is truly made complete in him. This is how we know we are in him: Whoever claims to live in him must walk as Jesus did" (1 John 1:5, 6).

Complacency, or deep satisfaction, in holiness or moral excellence is another attribute of benevolence, or love. This consists in benevolence contemplated in its relations to holy beings.

Complacency also expresses a state both of the intelligence and of the sensibility. Moral agents by nature necessarily approve of moral worth or excellence. And when even sinners behold right character or moral goodness, they are compelled to respect and approve it by a law of their intelligence. This they very often regard as evidence of goodness in themselves. But this is doubtless just as common in hell as it is on earth. The worst sinners on earth or in hell have, by the unalterable constitution of their nature, the necessity imposed upon them of paying *intellectual homage* to moral excellence. When a moral agent is intensely contemplating moral excellence, and his intellectual approval is emphatically pronounced, the natural (and often the necessary) result is a corresponding feeling of complacency or delight in the emotions. But since feeling is altogether an involuntary state of mind, it has no moral character. Complacency as a phenomenon of will has moral character when a moral being wills the actual highest blessedness of the holy being as a good in itself and solely because of his moral excellence.

This attribute as a phenomenon of the will is the cause of a complacent state of the sensibility, or emotions. It is true that feelings of complacency may exist when the will is not involved. But complacency of feeling surely will exist when complacency of will exists. Complacency of *will* implies complacency of *conscience* or the approval that the mind clearly recognizes. When there is a complacency of intelligence and of will, there will of course be complacency of the emotions.

In the common language of Christians and often in the popular language of the Bible, complacency of feeling is that which is generally termed *love* to God and to the saints. It is a vivid and pleasant state of the emotions, and of course very noticeable consciously. Indeed, it is perhaps the general usage now to call this phenomenon of the emotions, *love,* and for lack of just discrimination to speak of it as constituting religion. Many seem to suppose that this feeling of delight in, and fondness for, God is the love required by the moral law.

Yet, these people are conscious of not being volitional in this feeling of love, as well they may be. They judge their religious state, not by the end or goal for which they live—that is, by their choice or intention—but by their *emotions.* If they find themselves strongly exercised with *emotions* of love to God, they look upon themselves as being in a state well pleasing to God. But if their feelings or emotions of love are not active, of course they judge themselves to have little or no religion. It is remarkable to what extent religion is regarded as a phenomenon of the emotions, consisting in mere feelings. So common is it, indeed, that almost uniformly when professed Christians speak of their *experience,* they speak of their *feelings* instead of speaking of their conscious consecration to God and to the good of being.

It is also somewhat common for them to speak of *their* views of Christ, and rightly so, in a manner that shows that they regard the states of the intelligence as constituting at least a part of their religion. It is very important that correct views should prevail among Christians on this significant subject.

Virtue or religion must be a phenomenon of the heart or will. The attribute of benevolence which we are considering—respect of heart or will toward God—is the most common light in which the Scriptures present it, and also the most common form in which it will be revealed in our consciousness. The Scriptures often assign the goodness of God as a reason for loving Him, and Christians are conscious of having much regard for His goodness in their love for Him. I mean in their goodwill to Him. They will good to Him and ascribe all praise and glory to Him upon the condition that He deserves it. Of this they are conscious.

Now, in their love or goodwill to God, they do not regard His goodness as the fundamental reason for willing good to Him. Although His goodness is that which at the time most strongly impresses their minds, yet it must be that the intrinsic value of His well-being is assumed by them, or they would no sooner will that than anything else to Him. In willing His good, they must assume its intrinsic value to Him as the fundamental reason for willing it, and His goodness as a secondary reason or condition. They are conscious of being influenced greatly in willing His good in particular because of a regard for His goodness. If you should ask the Christian why he loved God or why he exercised goodwill to God, he would probably reply, "It is because God is good." But suppose he were further asked why he willed good rather than evil to God, he would say, "Because good is good or valuable to God." Or if he returned the same answer as at first, that is, because God is good, he would give this answer only because he would think it impossible for anyone not to assume and to know that good is willed instead of evil because of its intrinsic value. The fact is, the intrinsic value of well-being is necessarily recognized by the mind, and always assumed by it as a first truth. When a virtuous being is perceived, this first truth being spontaneously and necessarily assumed, the mind thinks only of the secondary reason or condition or the virtue of the being in willing good to Him.

The philosophy of the heart's complacency in God may be illustrated by many familiar examples. For instance, the law of cause and effect is a first truth. Everyone assumes it and must assume it. No one ever can *practically* deny it. Suppose I have some important goal to accomplish. In looking around for a way to accomplish my goal, I discover a certain method which I am sure will accomplish it. It is the tendency of this method to accomplish my goal that influences my thinking at the time. If I were asked why I chose this method, I would naturally answer, "Because of its utility or tendency." I would be clearly aware of the reason for choosing such a method. But it is perfectly plain that the fundamental reason for this choice, and one which was assumed (and had in fact the prime and fundamental influence in producing the choice), was the intrinsic value of the end to which the thing chosen sustained the relation of a means. Every choice I make is to achieve some goal or ultimate end.

Take another illustration: a first truth is that happiness is intrinsically valuable. Everybody knows and assumes it as such. Suppose I see a virtuous character. Assuming the first truth that happiness is intrinsically valuable, I affirm irresistibly that God deserves happiness and that it is my duty to will God's happiness. Now, in this case the affirmation that God deserves happiness and I ought to will it is based upon the assumption that happiness is intrinsically valuable—valuable in itself and for its own sake.

The thing with which I am immediately conscious of influencing me, and which necessitated the affirmation of the obligation to will His good, and which induced me to will it, was that I perceived in God's goodness His right to happiness. Nevertheless, it is certain that I did assume, and was fundamentally influenced both in my affirmation of obligation and in my choice of the first truth, that happiness is intrinsically valuable. I assumed it and was influenced by it, though unconscious of it. And this is generally true of first truths. They are so universally and so necessarily assumed in practice that we lose the direct consciousness of their influence on us. Myriads of illustrations of this are arising all around us. We really do love God; that is, we exercise goodwill to Him. Of this we are strongly conscious. We are also conscious of willing His actual blessedness because He is good. This reason we naturally assign to ourselves and others. But in this we may overlook the fact that there is still another deeper and more fundamental reason assumed for willing His good, that is, its intrinsic value. And this reason is so fundamental that we should irresistibly affirm our obligation to will His good upon the bare perception of His susceptibility of happiness wholly irrespective of His character.

Before I close this subject, I must refer again to the matter of complacent love as a phenomenon of the emotions and also as a phenomenon of the intelligence. There are sad mistakes and gross and ruinous delusions entertained by many regarding this subject. The intelligence by necessity perfectly approves of the character of God as it understands it. The intelligence is so correlated to the feelings that where it clearly perceives the divine excellence, or the excellence of the divine law, the emotions are affected by the perception of the intelligence as a thing of course and necessity. Emotions of complacency and delight in the law and in the divine character, therefore, may often glow and burn in the emotions while the heart or will is unaffected. The will remains in a selfish choice while the intellect and the emotions are strongly impressed with the perception of the Divine excellence. No doubt this state of the intellect and the feelings are often mistaken for true religion. We have clear illustrations of this in the Bible, and great multitudes of cases of it in common life. "Yet they seek me daily, and delight to know my ways, as a nation that did righteousness, and forsook not the ordinance of their God: they ask of me the ordinance of justice, they take delight in approaching to God" (Isa. 58:2). "And, lo, thou art unto them as a very lovely song of one that hath a pleasant voice, and can play well on an instrument: for they hear thy words, but they do them not" (Ezek. 33:32).

Nothing is of greater importance than to forever understand that religion is always and necessarily a phenomenon of the will, that it always and necessarily produces outward action and inward feeling. On account of the correlation of the intellect and the emotions, almost every variety of feeling may exist in the mind as produced by the perceptions of the intelligence regardless of the state of the will. Unless we are conscious of goodwill or of consecration to God and the good of being, of living for this goal, it avails us nothing, whatever our views and feelings may be.

Let us reiterate that although these views and feelings may exist while the heart is wrong, they will certainly exist when the heart is right. There may be feeling, even deep feeling, when the heart is wrong. Yet there will and must be deep emotion and strenuous action when the heart is right. Let it be remembered, then, that complacency as a phenomenon of the will is always a striking characteristic of true love or benevolence to God; that is, that the mind is affected and consciously influenced in willing the actual and infinite blessedness of God because of a regard to His goodness. The goodness of God is not, as has been repeatedly shown, the fundamental influence or reason of the goodwill. It is one reason or a condition both of the possibility of willing and of the obligation to will His actual blessedness. It assigns to itself and to others, as has been said, this reason for loving God, or willing His good, rather than the truly fundamental one—that is, the intrinsic value of good—because that is so universally and so necessarily assumed that it thinks not of mentioning that, taking it always for granted that that will and must be understood.

FOR REFLECTION

God deserves my loving dedication to Him, and I consecrate myself to serving Him with all my abilities. I don't simply appreciate God for who He is and for what He has done, and then call these good feelings Christian love or true religion. I have chosen to further His Kingdom. That is my expression of Christian love and true religion.

9

LOVE IS COURAGEOUS

"Do not love the world or anything in the world. If anyone loves the world, the love of the Father is not in him. For everything in the world—the cravings of the sinful man, the lust of his eyes and the boasting of what he has and does—comes not from the Father but from the world. The world and its desires pass away, but the man who does the will of God lives forever" (1 John 2:15–17).

Opposition to sin is another attribute or characteristic of true love to God.

Opposition to sin is simply benevolence manifested in its relationships to sin. This attribute of love certainly is implied in the very essence and nature of benevolence. Benevolence is good willing, or willing the highest good of being as an end. Now, there is nothing in the universe more flagrantly and diametrically opposite to this end than sin. Benevolence cannot do otherwise than be forever opposed to sin as that abominable thing which it necessarily hates. It is absurd and a contradiction to affirm that benevolence is not opposed to sin. God is love, or benevolence. He must, therefore, be the unalterable opponent of sin—of all sin, in every form and degree.

But there is a state, both of the intellect and of the emotions, that is often mistaken for the opposition of the will to sin. Opposition to sin as a virtue is and must be a phenomenon of the will. But it also often exists as a phenomenon of the intellect and likewise of the emotions. The intelligence cannot contemplate sin without disapproval. This disapproval is often mistaken for opposition by the heart or will. When the intellect strongly disapproves of and denounces sin, there is naturally and necessarily a corresponding feeling of opposition to it in the feelings, an emotion of loathing, of hatred, of abhorrence. This is often mistaken for opposition by the will or heart. This is manifest from the fact that often the most notorious sinners manifest strong indignation in view of oppression, injustice, falsehood, and many other forms of sin. This phenomenon of the emotions and of the intellect, as I said, is often mistaken for a virtuous opposition to sin.

But remember that the only virtuous opposition to sin is a phenomenon of the will. Virtuous opposition to sin is a characteristic of love to God and man, or a characteristic of benevolence. This opposition to sin cannot possibly coexist with any degree of sin in the heart. That is, opposition to sin cannot coexist with a sinful choice. The will cannot at the same time be opposed to sin and commit sin. This is impossible. The very supposition that one can commit sin and be opposed to sin at the same time involves a contradiction. Opposition to sin as a phenomenon of the intellect or of the emotions may exist: the intellect may strongly disapprove of sin, and the emotions may be strongly opposed to sin, while at the same time the will may cleave to self-indulgence, or to that which constitutes sin. This fact, no doubt, accounts for the common mistake some hold that we can at the same time have a virtuous opposition to sin and still continue to commit sin.

Many are laboring under this fatal delusion. They are conscious not only of an intellectual disapproval of sin, but also at times of strong feelings of opposition to sin. And yet they are also conscious of continuing to commit sin. They therefore conclude that they have a principle of holiness in themselves, and also a principle of sin: that they are partly holy and partly sinful at the same time. They suppose their opposition of intellect and feeling to be a holy opposition, when no doubt it is just as common in hell, and even more so than it is on earth because sin is more naked there than it generally is here.

But now some may ask, "How is it that both the intellect and the emotions are opposed to sin, and yet it is persevered in? What reason can the mind have for a sinful choice when it is not encouraged either by the intellect or the emotions?" The philosophy of this phenomenon needs explanation.

I am a moral agent. My intelligence necessarily disapproves of sin. My feelings are so correlated to my intellect that they sympathize with it, or are affected by its perceptions and its judgments. I contemplate sin. I necessarily disapprove and condemn it. This affects my feelings. I loathe and abhor it. I nevertheless commit it. Now, how is this to be accounted for? The usual method is by ascribing it to a depravity in the will itself, a lapsed or corrupted state of the faculty so that it perversely chooses sin for its own sake. Although disapproved by the intelligence and loathed by the feelings, yet such, it is said, is the inherent depravity of the will that it tenaciously cleaves to sin notwithstanding. Further, it will continue to do so until the faculty is renewed by the Holy Spirit and a holy bias or inclination is impressed upon the will itself.

This is a gross mistake. In order to see the truth on this subject, it is extremely important to define what sin is.

All people admit that selfishness is sin. Comparatively few seem to understand that selfishness is the sum total of sin, and that every form of sin is an aspect of selfishness, just as every form of virtue is an aspect of benevolence. It is not my purpose now to show that selfishness is the sum total of sin. It is sufficient for the present to declare that selfishness is sin. But what is selfishness? Selfishness is the choice of self-gratification as an end. It is the preference of our own desires to the highest good of universal being. Self-gratification is the supreme end of selfishness. This choice is sinful. That is, the moral element, quality or attribute of this selfish choice is sin. In no case can sin be chosen for its own sake or as an end. Whenever anything is chosen to gratify self, it is not chosen because the choice is sinful. Nevertheless, it is sinful. The choice does not focus on the sinfulness of the choice as an end or for its own sake, but rather the gratification which will be attained by the thing chosen. For example, theft is sinful. The will, however, in an act of theft does not aim at and terminate on the sinfulness of theft, but upon the gratification expected from the stolen object. Drunkenness is sinful, but the drunkard does not intend or choose the sinfulness for its own sake or as an end. He does not choose strong drink because the choice is sinful, which it is, but rather for the gratification attained. We choose the gratification, but not the sin, as the end. To choose the gratification as an end is sinful, but it is not the sin that is the object of choice.

Our mother Eve ate the forbidden fruit. But the thing she chose or intended was not the sinfulness of eating but the gratification expected from the fruit. It is not, it cannot in any case be true that sin is chosen as an end or for its own sake. Sin is only a quality of selfishness. Selfishness is the choice, not of sin as an end for its own sake, but of self-gratification; and this choice of self-gratification as an end is sinful. That is, the moral element, quality or attribute of the choice is sin. To say that sin is or can be chosen for its own sake is absurd. It is the same as saying that a choice can terminate on an element, quality or attribute of itself; that the thing chosen is really an element of the choice itself. This is absurd.

But some say that sinners are sometimes conscious of choosing sin for its own sake, or because it is sin. They say they possess such a malicious state of mind that they love sin for its own sake; that they "roll sin as a sweet morsel under their tongue." Further, "they eat up the sins of God's people as they eat bread"—that is, they love their sins and the sins of others as they do their necessary food, and choose it for that reason, just as they do their food. They themselves not only sin with greediness, but also have pleasure in those who do sin. Now all this may be true, yet it does not disprove in any way the position which I have taken—that sin never is and never can be chosen as an end, or for its own sake. Sin may be sought and loved as a means, but never as an end.

The choice of food will illustrate this. Food is never chosen as an ultimate end: it never can be chosen for this reason. Choosing food is always a means to an end. It is the gratification or the use of it in some way or other that determines the reason for choosing it. Gratification is always the end for which a selfish person eats. It may not be merely the present pleasure of eating which is his primary motive. Nevertheless, if he is a selfish person, he has his own gratification in view as an end. It may be that it is not so much a present as a remote gratification he has in view. Thus, he may choose food to give him health and strength to pursue some distant gratification, the acquisition of wealth or something else that will gratify him.

It may happen that a sinner may get into such an alarming state of rebellion against God and the universe that he will take pleasure in willing and in doing and saying things that are sinful because they are sinful and displeasing to God and to holy beings. But in this case, sin is not chosen as an end, but as a means of gratifying this malicious feeling. It is, after all, self-gratification that is chosen as an end, and not sin. Sin is the means, and self-gratification is the end.

Now we are prepared to understand how it can be that both the intellect and the emotions can often be opposed to sin, and yet the will cleave to the indulgence. Take for example a drunkard who contemplates the moral character of drunkenness. He instantly and necessarily condemns the abomination. His feelings sympathize with the intellect. He loathes not only the sinfulness of drinking liquor, but also himself. He is ashamed, and were it possible, he would spit in his own face. Now in this state it would surely be absurd to suppose that he could choose the sin of drinking as an end, or *for its own sake*. This would be choosing it for an impossible reason. But he still might choose to continue drinking, not because it is sinful, even though it is. For while the intellect condemns the sin of drinking liquor, and the emotions loathe the sinfulness of the indulgence, nevertheless, there still exists so strong an appetite (not for the sin, but for the liquor) that the will seeks the gratification regardless of its sinfulness.

So it is in every case where sin is committed in the face of the protests of the intelligence and the loathing of the emotions. The emotions loathe the sinfulness, but more strongly desire the thing, and such a choice is sinful. The will in a selfish being yields to the strongest impulse of the feelings, and the end chosen is in no case sin, but self-gratification. Those who suppose this opposition of the intellect or of the emotions to be a holy principle are fatally deluded. This kind of opposition to sin, as I have said before, is doubtless common and always must be in hell. It is this kind of opposition to sin that often manifests itself among wicked men, and that leads them to take credit for goodness which they do not possess. They will not believe themselves to be morally and totally depraved while they are conscious of so much hostility to sin within them. But they should understand that this opposition is not of the will or they could not continue in sin. It is purely an involuntary state of mind, and has no moral character whatever. Let it be ever remembered, then, that a virtuous opposition to sin is always and necessarily an attribute of benevolence, a phenomenon of the will, and that it is naturally impossible for this opposition of will to coexist with the practice of sin.

As opposition to sin is plainly implied in and is an essential attribute of benevolence, or true love to God, it follows that obedience to the law of God cannot be partial in the sense that we can both love God and sin at the same time.

Opposition to benevolence, or to virtue or to holiness and true religion, is one of the attributes of selfishness.

In its relations to benevolence, selfishness is not a mere negation. It is the choice of self-gratification as the supreme and ultimate purpose of life. If the will is committed to selfishness, and contemplation of committing the mind to benevolence begins, the will cannot remain in a state of indifference to benevolence. It must either yield its preference for self-indulgence, or resist the benevolence which the intellect perceives. The will cannot continue in exercising this selfish choice without, as it were, bracing and girding itself against that virtue which it does not imitate. If it does not imitate it, it must be because it refuses to do so. The intelligence does and must strongly urge the will to imitate benevolence and to seek the same end. The will must yield or resist, and the resistance must be more or less resolute and determined as the demands of the intelligence dictate. This resistance to benevolence, or to the demands of the intelligence, is what the Bible calls hardening of the heart. Hardening of the heart is obstinacy of the will under the light of the presence of true religion and the claims of benevolence.

Unless selfishness is abandoned, opposition to benevolence or true religion must be developed whenever the mind apprehends true religion. Not only must this opposition be developed, or selfishness abandoned under such circumstances, but it must increase as true religion displays more and more of its loveliness. As the light from the radiant sun of benevolence is poured more and more upon the darkness of selfishness, the opposition of the heart must of necessity increase in the same proportion, or selfishness must be abandoned. Selfishness which remains under light must manifest more and more opposition in proportion to the increasing light which strips the soul of any excuse for opposing it.

This characteristic of selfishness has always been manifested proportionately whenever it has been exposed by the light of true religion. This accounts for all the opposition to true religion since the world began. It also proves that where there are impenitent sinners, and they retain their impenitence and manifest no hostility to the religion which they witness, there is something defective in the professed piety which they see, or at least they do not contemplate all the attributes of true piety. It also proves that persecution will always exist where true religion is manifested to those who cling to their selfishness.

The fact is that selfishness and benevolence are just as much opposed to each other and as necessarily at war with each other as God and Satan, as heaven and hell. There can never be a truce between them; they are essential and eternal opposites. They are not merely opposites; they are opposite causes. They are essential activities. They are the two, and the only two, great antagonistic principles in the universe of mind. Each is heaving and energizing like a volcano to attain its end. A war of mutual and uncompromising extermination necessarily exists between them. Neither can tolerate the presence of the other without repellence and opposition. Each energizes to subdue and overcome the other; and selfishness already has shed an ocean of the blood of the saints, and also the precious blood of the Prince of life. There is not a more gross and injurious mistake than to suppose that selfishness under any circumstances ever becomes reconciled to benevolence. The supposition is absurd and contradictory; for selfishness to become reconciled to benevolence, selfishness would have to become benevolence. Selfishness may change the mode of attack or its opposition against benevolence, but its real opposition can never change while it retains its own nature and continues to be selfishness. Love must be courageous in its opposition to selfishness.

The opposition of the heart to benevolence often produces deep opposition to feeling. The opposition of the will causes the intellect to fabricate excuses, objections, lies, refuges, and often greatly perverts the thoughts, and produces the most bitter feelings imaginable toward God and toward the saints. Selfishness will strive to justify its opposition and to shield itself against the reproaches of conscience, and will resort to every possible means to cover up its real hostility to holiness. It will pretend that it is not holiness but sin that it opposes. But the fact is, it is not sin but holiness to which it stands forever opposed. The opposition of feeling is only developed when the heart is exposed to strong moral light and exercises deep and strong resistance. In such cases the emotions sometimes boil with feelings of bitter opposition to God and Christ and to all good.

The question is often asked, May not this opposition exist in the emotional realm with feelings of hostility to God even though the heart is in a truly benevolent state? To this inquiry I reply: If it can it must be produced by infernal or some other influence that misrepresents God and places His character before the mind in a false light. Blasphemous thoughts may be suggested or injected into the mind. These thoughts may have their natural effect in the emotions, and feelings of bitterness and hostility may exist without the consent of the will. The will may all the while be endeavoring to repel these suggestions, and divert the attention from such thoughts, yet Satan may continue to hurl his fiery darts, and the soul may be racked with torture under the poison of hell, which seems to be taking effect in the emotions. The mind, at such times, seems to itself to be filled, so far as feeling is concerned, with all the bitterness of hell. And so it is, and yet it may be, that in all this there is no selfishness. If the will holds fast its integrity; if it holds out in the struggle, and where God is maligned and misrepresented by the infernal suggestions, it says with Job, "Although he slay me, yet will I trust in him," no selfishness has occurred. However sharp the conflict in such cases, we can look back and say that we are more than conquerors through Christ who loves us. In such cases it is the selfishness of Satan and not our own selfishness that kindled up those fires of hell in our emotions. The Bible says, "Blessed is he that endureth temptation; for when he is tried he shall have a crown of life" (James 1:12). Love must be courageous in the battle against sin, temptation, and the devil.

FOR REFLECTION

I will not commit the same sins over and over again, I will believe that in Christ I have power over them. I will not follow the suggestions of Satan or gratify my emotional drives in an unlawful or selfish manner.

10

LOVE IS COMPASSIONATE

"Suppose a brother or sister is without clothes and daily food. If one of you says to him, 'Go, I wish you well; keep warm and well fed,' but does nothing about his physical needs, what good is it?" (James 2:15, 16).

Compassion for the miserable is also an attribute of benevolence or of pure love to God and man. This is benevolence viewed in its relationships to misery and guilt.

There is also a compassion which is a phenomenon of the sensibility or feelings. It may and does often exist in the form of an emotion. But this emotion being involuntary has no moral character in itself. The compassion which is a virture and which is required of us as a duty is a phenomenon of the will, and is of course an attribute of benevolence. Benevolence is good willing or willing the highest happiness and well-being of God and the universe for its own sake or as an end. It is impossible from its own nature that compassion for the miserable should not be one of its attributes. When compassion of will exists, its choice toward misery is that it should not exist. Benevolence wills that happiness should exist for its own sake. This attribute or characteristic of benevolence consists in willing the happiness of the one who is miserable. Benevolence, therefore, is simply willing the good or happiness of being in general. Compassion of will is a willing that the miserable, in particular, should be happy.

Compassion of sensibility is a feeling of pity in view of misery. As has been said, it is not a virtue. It is only a desire, not a choice. Consequently, it does not benefit its object. It is the state of mind of which James speaks. This kind of compassion may consist and coexist with selfishness. But compassion of heart or will cannot, because it consists in willing the happiness of the one who is miserable for its own sake and of course impartially. It will, and from its very nature must, deny self to promote its end whenever it wisely can; that is, when it is demanded by the highest general good. Circumstances may exist that may render it unwise to express this compassion by actually extending relief to the miserable. Such circumstances forbid that God should extend relief to the lost in hell. If it weren't because of their character and moral governmental relationships, God's compassion would no doubt make immediate efforts for their relief.

Although many circumstances may exist in which compassion would hasten to the relief of its object, yet on the whole the misery that exists is regarded as the lesser of two evils. Therefore, the *wisdom* of benevolence forbids it to reach out and save its object.

It is very important to distinguish carefully between compassion as a phenomenon of the sensibility or as a mere *feeling*, and compassion considered as a phenomenon of the *will*. This, remember, is the only form of virtuous compassion. Many who naturally feel quickly and deeply often take credit for being compassionate, while they seldom extend help to the poor, the down-trodden, and the miserable. Their compassion is a mere feeling. It says, "Be warmed and clothed," but does not provide for the person's need.

The will is often influenced by the *feeling of compassion*. In this case, the mind is no less selfish in seeking to promote the relief and happiness of its object than it is in any other form of selfishness. In such cases, self-gratification is the end sought, and the relief of the suffering is only a means. Pity is stirred, and deep feelings of pain are aroused by the contemplation of misery. The will is influenced by this feeling, and makes efforts to relieve the painful emotion on the one hand, and to gratify the desire to see the sufferer happy on the other. This is only an imposing form of selfishness. We, no doubt, often witness this exhibition of self-gratification. The happiness of the miserable is not in this case sought as an end or for its own sake, but as a means of gratifying our own feelings. This is not obedience of will to the law of intelligence, but obedience to the impulse of the emotions. It is not rational and intelligent compassion, but the same compassion as we often see mere animals exercise. They will risk, and even lay down their lives, to give relief to one of their own kind or to a person who is in misery. In them this has no moral character. Having no reason, it is not sin for them to obey their feelings. On the contrary, this is the law of their being. This they cannot help but do. For them, then, to seek their own gratification as an end is not sin. But people have reason, and they are bound to obey it. People should will and seek the relief and the happiness of those who are miserable for its own sake or for its own intrinsic value. When a person tries to seek another's happiness for no higher reason than to gratify his own feelings, he denies his humanity. He seeks it, not out of regard for the one suffering, but in self-defense, or to relieve his own pain and to gratify his own desires. This is sin.

Many people, who take much credit for benevolence, are actually only exercising this imposing form of selfishness. They take credit for holiness when their holiness is only sin. What is especially worthy of notice here is that this class of people appear to themselves and to others to be all the more virtuous by how much more manifestly and exclusively they are led on by the impulse of feelings. They are conscious of feeling deeply, of being most sincere and earnest in obeying their feelings. Everybody who knows them can also see that they feel deeply and are influenced by the strength of their feelings rather than by their intelligence. Most people are so totally deceived on this subject that they award praise to themselves and to others in proportion to the certainty they have in being motivated by the depth of their feelings rather than by their sober judgment.

But I must not leave this subject without also observing that when compassion exists as a phenomenon of the *will* it will also certainly exist as a feeling of the sensibility. A person with a compassionate heart will also be a person with compassionate sensibility. He will feel and he will act. Nevertheless, his actions will not be the effect of his feelings, but will be the result of his sober judgment.

These classes see themselves and are generally seen by others to be truly compassionate people. The one class exhibit much feeling of compassion, but their compassion does not influence their will; hence, they do not act for the relief of suffering. These content themselves with mere desires and tears. They say, "Be warmed and clothed," but do not give the needed relief. Another class feel deeply, and give in to their feelings. Of course they are active and energetic in the relief of suffering. But being governed by feeling, instead of being influenced by their intelligence, they are not virtuous but selfish. Their compassion is only an imposing form of selfishness. A third class feel deeply, but are not governed by blind impulses of feeling. They take a rational view of the subject and act wisely and energetically. They obey their reason. Their feelings do not lead them, and they do not seek to gratify their feelings. Those in this last group are truly virtuous, and above all the most happy of the three. Their feelings are all the more gratified by how much less they aim at the gratification. They obey their intelligence, and therefore have the double satisfaction of the applause of conscience while their feelings are also fully gratified by seeing their desire accomplished.

The opposite of this is *cruelty* which is an attribute of selfishness. It is often used to designate a state of the emotions, and represents that state of feeling that has a barbarous or savage pleasure in the misery of others.

Cruelty as a phenomenon of the *will* or as an attribute of selfishness has two characteristics. First, it is a reckless disregard of the well-being of God and the universe; and secondly, it perseveres in a course that must ruin the souls of the subjects under it, and so far as they have influence, the souls of others.

What should we think of a person who was so intent on attaining some petty gratification that he would not give the alarm if a city were on fire and the sleeping citizens in imminent danger of perishing in the flames! Suppose that instead of denying himself some momentary gratification he would rather jeopardize many lives. Should we not call this cruelty? Now, there are many forms of cruelty. Because sinners are not always brought into circumstances where they exercise certain forms of it, they flatter themselves that they are not cruel. But the fact is that selfishness is always cruel—cruel to the soul and highest interests of the one who suffers from it. Selfishness is cruel to the souls of others in neglecting to do for their salvation what may be done, cruel to God in abusing Him in ten thousand ways, and cruel to the whole universe. If we should be shocked at the cruelty of one who might see his neighbor's house on fire, and the family asleep, and neglect to give them warning because he is too self-indulgent to rise from his bed, what shall we say of the cruelty of one who sees his neighbor's soul in peril of eternal death, and yet neglects to give him warning!

Sinners are apt to possess very good dispositions, as they express it. They suppose they are the opposite of being cruel. They possess tender feelings and are often very compassionate toward those who are sick, in distress, or suffering affliction of any kind. They are ready to do many things for them. Such people would be shocked if they were called cruel. Many who profess to be Christians would take their part and consider them abused. Of all their attributes, cruelty is not one of them. Now, it is true that there are certain forms of cruelty of which such people are not guilty. But this is only because God has so molded their nature that they are not delighted in the misery of their fellowmen. However, there is no virtue in their not being gratified at the sight of suffering, nor in their effort to prevent it while they continue selfish. They follow the impulses of their feelings, and if their temperament were such that it would gratify them to inflict misery on others, their selfishness would instantly take on that type. Though cruelty in all its forms is not common to all selfish people, it is still true that some form of cruelty is practiced by every sinner. God says, "The tender mercies of the wicked are cruel" (Prov. 12:10). The fact that they live in sin, that they set an example of selfishness, that they do nothing for their own souls or for the souls of others—these are really atrocious forms of cruelty. They infinitely exceed all those comparatively petty forms that relate to the miseries of people in this life.

FOR REFLECTION

My efforts to bring relief to the starving and needy people of the world are not motivated simply by the emotional pull on my heart of sly advertising appeals. I reasonably seek to meet the needs of others in the best possible ways available to me. I seek to win others to God in Christ.

11

LOVE IS MERCIFUL

"Blessed are the merciful, for they will be shown mercy" (Matt. 5:7).

Mercy is an attribute of benevolence. And this term likewise expresses a state of feeling and represents a phenomenon of the emotions. Mercy is often understood to be synonymous with compassion, but then it is not rightly understood.

Mercy, considered as a phenomenon of the will, is a disposition to pardon crime. It consists in willing the pardon and the well-being of one who deserves punishment. It is goodwill viewed in relationship to one who deserves punishment. Mercy, considered as a feeling or phenomenon of the emotions, is a desire for the pardon or good of one who deserves punishment. It is only a feeling, a desire. It is definitely involuntary and in itself has no moral character.

Mercy, as an attribute of benevolence, or love, is willing the pardon and the good of the culprit. It will, of course, manifest itself in action and in effort to pardon or to procure a pardon unless the attribute of wisdom prevents it. It may be unwise to pardon or to seek the pardon of someone who is guilty. In such cases, as all the attributes of benevolence must necessarily harmonize, no effort will be made to attain its end.

It was this attribute of benevolence modified and limited in its exercise by wisdom and justice that energized in providing the means and in opening the way for the pardon of our guilty race.

As wisdom and justice are also attributes of benevolence, mercy can never manifest itself by efforts to secure its end except in a manner and under conditions that do not set aside wisdom and justice. No one attribute of benevolence can be exercised at the expense of or in opposition to another attribute. The moral attributes of God, as has been said, are only attributes of benevolence, for benevolence embraces and expresses the sum total of them. From the term benevolence we learn that the end upon which it focuses is good. And we must also infer that the means are acceptable, because it is absurd to suppose that good would be chosen because it is good, and yet that the mind that makes this choice should not hesitate to use objectionable and harmful means to obtain its end. It would be a contradiction to will good for its own sake or out of regard to its intrinsic value, and then choose harmful means to accomplish this end. This cannot be. The mind that can focus on the highest well-being of God and the universe as an end can never consent to use efforts for the accomplishment of this end that are inconsistent with it, that is, that tend to prevent the highest good of being.

Mercy, as I have said, is that attribute of benevolence that wills the pardon of the guilty. But this attribute cannot be exercised in violation with the other attributes of benevolence. Mercy viewed by itself would pardon without repentance or condition, without reference to public justice. But viewed in its relationships with the other attributes of benevolence, we learn that although it is a real attribute of benevolence, mercy is not and cannot be exercised without the fulfillment of those conditions that will be in harmony with all the other attributes of benevolence.

This truth is beautifully taught and illustrated in the doctrine and fact of the atonement. Indeed, without consideration of the various attributes of benevolence, we are necessarily all in the dark and in confusion in respect to the character and government of God; the spirit and meaning of the law; the spirit and meaning of the gospel; our own spiritual state, and the developments of character around us. Without a knowledge of the attributes of love, or benevolence, we will be perplexed by apparent discrepancies in the Bible and in the Divine administration—and in the manifestations of Christian character both as revealed in the Bible and as exhibited in everyday life.

Take for example how universalists have stumbled because they do not thoroughly understand this subject! To them, God is love! They do not think about the attributes of this love of God, they infer that if God is love, He cannot hate sin and sinners. If He is merciful, He cannot punish sinners in hell. Unitarians have stumbled in the same way. They reason that since God is merciful—that is, disposed to pardon sin—what need is there for an atonement? If He is merciful, He can and will pardon upon repentance without atonement. But we may inquire, if He is merciful, why not pardon without repentance? If His mercy alone is the only motivating factor to pardon, then there is no need to wait for repentance. But if repentance is and must be a condition of the exercise of mercy, then there must be other conditions for its exercise. If wisdom and public justice are also attributes of benevolence and condition the exercise of mercy, and forbid that it should be exercised unless repentance is evident, why don't they equally condition its exercise upon such a satisfaction of public justice as would produce as full and as deep a respect for the law as the execution of its penalty would do? In other words, if wisdom and justice are attributes of benevolence, and condition the exercise of mercy upon repentance, why don't they also condition its exercise upon the fact of an atonement? Since mercy is an attribute of benevolence, it will naturally and inevitably direct the attention of the intellect to devising ways and means to render the exercise of mercy consistent with the other attributes of benevolence. It will employ the intelligence in devising means to ensure the repentance of the sinner, and to remove all the obstacles out of the way of its free and full exercise.

Mercy will also produce the state of feeling which is also called mercy or compassion. Hence it is certain that mercy will bring about efforts to procure the repentance and pardon of sinners. It will produce a deep yearning in the emotions over them, and energetic action to accomplish its end, that is, to bring about their repentance and pardon. This attribute of benevolence led the Father to give His only begotten and well-beloved Son, and it led the Son to give himself to die to secure the repentance and pardon of sinners. It is this attribute of benevolence that leads the Holy Spirit to make such mighty and protracted efforts to bring about the repentance in sinners. It is also this attribute that energized the prophets, apostles and martyrs, and saints of every age, to secure the conversion of those lost in sin. It is an amiable attribute. All its sympathies are sweet and tender and kind as heaven.

The opposite of this is *unmercifulness* which is an attribute of selfishness. Mercy is a disposition to pardon crime, and will and must manifest itself in efforts to produce the conditions upon which crime can be reasonably forgiven, if such conditions can be obtained. Unmercifulness is an unwillingness to forgive sin, and of course manifests itself either by resisting efforts to guarantee its forgiveness, or by treating such efforts with coldness or contempt. The manner in which sinners treat the plan of salvation, the atonement of Christ, the means used by God and the Church to bring about the pardon of sin, demonstrates that their tender mercies are cruelty. The Apostle charges them with being "implacable, unmerciful" (Rom. 1:31). Their opposition to the gospel, to revivals of religion, and to all the exhibitions of the mercy of God which He has shown to our world show that unmercifulness is an attribute of their character.

Sinners generally profess to be the friends of mercy. With their lips they extol the mercy of God. But how do they treat it? Do they embrace it? Do they honor it as something which they favor? Do they hold it forth to all men as worthy of all acceptance? Or do they wage an unrelenting war with it? How did they treat Christ when He came on His errand of mercy? They appallingly demonstrated that unmercifulness was an essential attribute of their character. They persecuted unto death the very impersonation and embodiment of mercy. And this same attribute of selfishness has always manifested itself under some form whenever a development and an exhibition of mercy has been made. Let the blood of prophets and apostles, of millions of martyrs, and above all, the blood of the God of mercy, speak. What is their united testimony? The perfection of unmercifulness is one of the essential and eternal attributes of selfishness.

Therefore, whenever a selfish being appears to be of a merciful disposition, it is only in appearance. His feelings may be sensitive, and he may often or always yield to them, but this is only selfishness. The only reason every sinner does not exhibit every appalling form of unmercifulness and cruelty is that God has so tempered his ability to feel and so surrounded him with influences as to modify the manifestation of selfishness and to develop other attributes more prominently than this. Unmerciful he is and must be while he remains in sin. To represent him as other than an unmerciful wretch is to misrepresent him, no matter who it is. That delicate female who would faint at the sight of blood! If she is a sinner, she is spurning and scorning the mercy of God. She lets others go down to hell unpardoned without an effort to secure their pardon. Is she anything else than unmerciful? No language can describe the hardness of her heart. The cup of salvation is presented to her lips by a Savior's bleeding hand. Nevertheless she dashes it from herself, and tramples its contents beneath her feet. It passes from lip to lip. But she offers no prayer that it may be accepted; or if she does, it is only the prayer of a hypocrite while she rejects it herself. No, with all her delicacy, her tender mercies are utter cruelty. With her own hands she crucifies the Son of God afresh and would put Him to open shame! What a monstrous thought! A woman murdering the Savior of the world! Her hands and garments all stained with blood! And call her merciful! Is there no shame at such misrepresentation?

FOR REFLECTION

I will be merciful, and seek for a means to bring the Good News of God's choice to pardon the sinner through the atonement of Jesus Christ. I will try to understand and share the beautiful balance that God maintains with all His attributes of love.

12

LOVE IS JUST

"God presented him as a sacrifice of atonement, through faith in his blood. He did this to demonstrate his justice, because in his forbearance he had left the sins committed beforehand unpunished—he did it to demonstrate his justice at the present time, so as to be just and the one who justifies the man who has faith in Jesus" (Rom. 3:25–26).

Justice is another attribute of love.

Justice also expresses a state of phenomenon of the emotions. As an attribute of benevolence it is the opposite of mercy when viewed in its relationships to crime. Justice is a disposition or willing to treat every moral agent according to his intrinsic worth of merit. In its relationships to crime, to the criminal, and to the public, it consists in willing the criminal's punishment according to law. Mercy would *pardon*; justice would *punish* for the public good.

Justice as a phenomenon of the emotions is a feeling that the guilty deserves punishment, and a desire that he may be punished. This is an involuntary feeling and has no moral character. It is often strongly excited, and is often the cause of mobs and popular commotions. When it takes over the control of the will, as it often does with sinners, it leads to taking the law into their own hands in which they use methods of executing vengeance which are so often appalling.

I have said that the mere desire has no moral character. But when the will is governed by this desire and yields itself up to seek its own gratification, this state of the will is selfishness seen in one of its most odious and frightful forms. Under the providence of God, however, this form of selfishness, like every other in its turn, is overruled for good, like earthquakes, tornadoes, pestilence, and war, to purify the moral elements of society and scourge away those moral nuisances with which communities are sometimes infested. Even war itself is often but an illustration of this.

Justice, as an attribute of benevolence, is virtue, and exhibits itself among various ways in the execution of the penalties of law and in support of public order.

There are several variations of this attribute. That is, it may and must be viewed under various aspects and in various relationships. One of these is *public justice*. This is a regard for public interests, and guarantees a just administration of law for the public good. It will in no case tolerate the execution of the penalty to be set aside unless something is done to support the authority of the law and the lawgiver. It also guarantees the just administration of rewards, and strictly looks after the public interests, always insisting that the greater interest shall prevail over the lesser; that private interest shall never set aside or prejudice a public one of greater value. Public justice is modified in its exercise by the attribute of mercy. It conditions the exercise of mercy, and mercy conditions its exercise. Mercy cannot, in keeping with this attribute, extend a pardon except on conditions of repentance, or something equivalent being rendered to the government such as restitution, etc. So on the other hand, justice is conditioned by mercy, and cannot, in keeping with that attribute, proceed to take vengeance when the highest good does not require it and when punishment can be eliminated without public loss. Thus these attributes mutually limit each other's exercise and render the whole character of benevolence perfect, systematical, and heavenly.

Justice is considered one of the sterner attributes of benevolence; but it is indispensable to complete or give a total picture of the entire circle of moral perfections. Although solemn and awful, and sometimes inexpressibly dreadful in its exercise, it is nevertheless one of the glorious variations and manifestations of benevolence. Benevolence without justice would be anything but morally lovely and perfect. It could not even be benevolence. This attribute of benevolence is quite evident in the character of God as revealed in His law, in His gospel, and sometimes most impressively by His providence.

It is also evident in the history of inspired men. The Psalms abound with expressions of this attribute. We find many prayers for the punishment of the wicked. Samuel hewed Agag in pieces, and David wrote profusely with expressions showing that the attribute of justice was strongly developed in his mind. The circumstances which he often experienced made it proper to express and manifest in various ways the spirit of this attribute. Many have stumbled at such prayers, expressions, and manifestations which I have alluded to. But this is because they do not truly understand this attribute. They have supposed that such exhibitions were inconsistent with a right spirit. "Oh," they say, "how unevangelical! How un-Christlike! How inconsistent with the sweet and heavenly spirit of Christ and the gospel!" But this is all a mistake. These prayers were dictated by the Spirit of Christ. Such exhibitions are only the manifestations of one of the essential attributes of benevolence. Those sinners deserved to die. It was for the greatest good that they should be made a public example. The spirit of inspiration knew this, and such prayers under these circumstances are only an expression of the mind and will of God. They are truly the spirit of justice pronouncing sentence upon them.

These prayers and similar things found in the Bible are no vindication of or justification for the spirit of fanaticism and denunciation that so often have taken shelter under them. Fanatics might as well burn cities and lay waste countries, and seek to justify themselves by an appeal to the destruction of the old world by the great flood and the destruction of Sodom and Gomorrah by fire and brimstone.

Retributive justice is another variation of this attribute. It is a disposition to give the offender the punishment which he deserves, because it is fit and proper that a moral agent should be dealt with according to his deeds.

Another variation of this attribute is *commercial justice*. This attribute wills exact equivalents and uprightness in business transactions.

Other variations of this attribute exist, but the foregoing may suffice to illustrate sufficiently the various departments over which this attribute presides.

The attribute of justice, though stern in its spirit and manifestations, is nevertheless one of prime importance in all governments of moral agents whether human or divine. Indeed, without it government could not exist. It is vain for certain philosophers to discredit this attribute, and to dispense with it in the administration of government. They will, if they try the experiment, find to their cost and confusion that no one attribute of benevolence can say to another, "I have no need of thee." In short, let any one attribute of benevolence be destroyed or overlooked, and you have destroyed its perfection, its beauty, its harmony, its propriety, its glory. It is no longer benevolence, but a sickly, inefficient, and limping sentimentalism that has no God, no virtue, no beauty, or form, or comeliness in it, that when we see it we should desire it.

Justice executes law. It aims to produce commercial honesty, public and private integrity, and tranquillity. It says to violence, disorder, and injustice, "Peace, be still," and brings about a great calm. We see the evidences and the illustrations of this attribute in the thunderings of Sinai and in the agony of Calvary. We hear it in the wail of a world when the fountains of the great deep were broken up, when the windows of heaven were opened, and the floods descended, and the population of a globe was swallowed up. We see its manifestations in the destruction of Sodom and Gomorrah; and lastly, we shall forever see its bright but awful and glorious displays in the dark and curling folds of that pillar of smoke of the torment of the damned that ascends up before God forever and ever.

Many seem to be afraid to contemplate justice as an attribute of benevolence. Any manifestation of it among men causes them to recoil and shudder as if they saw a demon. But let it have its place in the glorious circle of moral attributes. It must have. It will have. It cannot be otherwise. Whenever any policy of government is adopted, in family or state, that excludes the exercise of this attribute, all will be failure, defeat, and ruin.

Justice being an attribute of benevolence will prevent the punishment of the finally impenitent sinner from taking away from the happiness of God and of holy beings. They will never delight in misery for its own sake. But they will take pleasure in the administration of justice. When the smoke of the torment of the damned comes up in the sight of heaven, they will, as they are represented, shout, "Alleluia! the Lord God Omnipotent reigneth. Just and righteous are thy ways thou King of saints!"

Where true benevolence exists, there must be exact justice, commercial or business honesty and integrity. This is a natural result of benevolence. The rendering of exact equivalents, or the intention to do so, must be a characteristic of a truly benevolent mind.

Impulsive benevolence may exist; that is, constitutional benevolence, falsely so called, may exist and yet justice will not exist. The mind may often be carried away by the impulse of feeling so that a man may at times have the appearance of true benevolence while the same individual is selfish in business, affecting all his commercial relationships. This has been an enigma to many, but the case is a plain one. The difficulty is the man is not just; that is, not truly benevolent. His benevolence is only another manifestation of selfishness. "He that hath an ear to hear, let him hear" (Rev. 2:7). His benevolence results from feeling and is not true benevolence because it does not originate in his will.

Where benevolence exists, the *Golden Rule* will surely be observed: "Whatsoever ye would that men should do to you, do ye even so to them" (Matt. 7:12). The justice of benevolence cannot fail to guarantee conformity to this rule. Benevolence is a just state of the will. It is a willing justly. It must then by a law of necessity produce a just outward behavior or lifestyle. If the heart is just, the life must be.

This attribute of benevolence will prevent one from displaying every kind and degree of injustice. He cannot be unjust to his neighbor's reputation, his person, his property, his soul, his body, nor indeed be unjust in any respect to God or man. It will produce confession and restitution in every case of remembered wrong, so far as this is practicable. It should be distinctly understood that a benevolent or a truly religious man cannot be unjust. He may indeed appear to be so to others; but he cannot be truly religious or benevolent and unjust at the same time. If at the time he is truly in a benevolent state of mind, and yet appears to be unjust in any instance, that *cannot be* the true evaluation for injustice cannot coexist in a truly benevolent state.

The attributes of selfishness, as we shall see in its proper place, are the direct opposite of those of benevolence. The two states of mind are as opposite as heaven and hell and can no more coexist in the same mind than a thing can be and not be at the same time. I said that if a person truly, in the exercise of benevolence, appears to be unjust in anything, he is only so in appearance and not in fact. *Remember*, I am speaking of one who is really in a benevolent state of mind at the time. He may mistake and do that which would be unjust if he sees it differently and intends differently. Justice and injustice belong to the intention, one's moral choices. No outward act can in itself be either just or unjust. To say that a person who is making and carrying out truly benevolent choices can at the same time be unjust is absurd. It is the same as saying that he can intend justly and unjustly at the same time and in regard to the same thing. This is a contradiction.

All along it must be remembered that benevolence is one identical thing, that is, goodwill, willing for its own sake the highest good of being and every known good according to its relative value. Consequently, justice must be an attribute of such a choice. Justice is regarding and treating, or rather willing everything just, in accord with its nature or intrinsic and relative value and relationships. To say, therefore, that present benevolence leaves room for any degree of present injustice is to affirm a veritable contradiction. A just person is a sanctified person, a perfect person, in the sense that he is at the present in a sinless state.

The direct opposite of this is *injustice* which is an attribute of selfishness.

Justice is a disposition to treat every being and interest according to its intrinsic worth. Injustice is the opposite of this. It is a disposition to prefer self-interest regardless of the relative value of the interests. The nature of selfishness demonstrates that injustice is always one of its attributes, and one that is universally and constantly manifested.

There is the utmost injustice in the end chosen. It is the practical preference of a petty self-interest over infinite interests. There is no other greater injustice than a universal injustice to God and man. It is the most obvious and most flagrant kind of injustice possible to every being in the universe. This selfish choice gives sufficient reason to anyone to charge him with the most flagrant and shocking injustice. This injustice affects every act every moment of his life. He is never in the least degree just to any being in the universe. He is perfectly unjust. He cares nothing for the rights of others as such, and never even in appearance regards them except for selfish reasons. This, then, can only be the appearance of regarding, for no right of any being in the universe can be respected by a selfish mind any further than in appearance. To deny this is to deny his selfishness. He performs no act except for one reason, that is, to promote his own gratification. This is his end, his supreme choice. For the realization of this end, every effort is made and every individual act and volition put forth. By remaining selfish, it is impossible for him to act in any other way. All his choices will directly or indirectly be made for this end. Because of the nature of selfishness, this end will be pursued in the most obvious and outrageous violation of the rights of God and of every creature in the universe. Justice demands that he should devote himself to the promotion of the highest good of God and the universe, that he should love God with all his heart and his neighbor as himself. Every sinner is openly, universally and as perfectly unjust as possible at every moment of his impenitence.

It should, therefore, always be understood that no sinner at any time is at all just to any being in the universe. All his paying of his debts, and all his apparent fairness and justice, is only a misleading form of selfishness. By the mere fact that he is a sinner, he has some selfish reason for all he does, is, says, or omits. His entire activity is selfishness, and while he remains impenitent, it is impossible for him to think, act, will, do, be, or say anything more or less than he sees expedient to promote his own interest. He is not just. He cannot be just, nor begin in any instance or the least way to be truly just either to God or man until he begins life anew, gives his heart to God, and consecrates his entire being to the promotion of the good of universal being. Justice demands this. There is no beginning to being just unless the sinner begins here. If you begin and continue to be just in the choice of the great end of life, then you will naturally be just in the use of means. But if you are unjust in the choice of an end, it is impossible for you, in any instance, to be otherwise than totally unjust in the use of means. In this case your entire activity is nothing else than a web of abominable injustices.

The only reason every sinner does not openly and daily practice every kind of outward commercial injustice is that he is in such a condition that upon the whole he judges that it is not in his selfish interests to practice those things. This is universally so. We owe no thanks to any sinner for abstaining in any instance from any kind or degree of injustice in practice, for he is restrained and kept from it only by selfish considerations. That is, he is too selfish to do it. His selfishness refrains him, not the love of God or man.

He may be hindered by an innate conscientiousness or sense of justice. But this is only a feeling, and if restrained only by this, he is just as absolutely selfish as if he had stolen a horse in obedience to the feeling of greed. God so tempers man's physical makeup as to restrain him; that is, that one form of selfishness shall prevail over another. The desire for approval and acceptance in most people is so large that to be applauded by their fellowmen so modifies the developments of their selfishness that they take on a type of outward decency and appearance of justice. But this is no less selfishness than if they took on a different type altogether.

FOR REFLECTION

I will remember that justice and mercy are both attributes of love in the way God deals with His creation, and He has called me to exercise both of these virtues in relationship with others under the prayerful empowerment of the Holy Spirit.

13

LOVE IS TRUTHFUL

"We know that we have come to know him if we obey his commands. The man who says, 'I know him,' but does not do what he commands is a liar, and the truth is not in him. But if anyone obeys his word, God's love is truly made complete in him. This is how we know we are in him: Whoever claims to live in him must walk as Jesus did" (1 John 2:3–6).

Truth, or *truthfulness,* is another attribute of love. Truth is both objective and subjective. Objective truth may be defined to be the reality of things, or how things really are. Truthfulness is subjective truth—the conformity of the will to the reality of things. Truth as stated is conformity of that statement to the reality of things. Truth in action is action conformed to the nature and relationships of things. Truthfulness is a disposition to conform to the reality of things. It is willing in accordance with the reality of things. It is *willing the right end by the right means.* It is willing the intrinsically valuable as an end and the relatively valuable as a means. In short, it is the willing of everything according to the reality or facts in the particular case.

Truthfulness, then, must be an attribute of benevolence. It is, like all the attributes, only benevolence manifested in a certain aspect or relationship. It cannot be distinguished from benevolence, for it is not distinct from it, but only a phase or form of benevolence. The universe is so constructed that if everything proceeds and is conducted and willed according to its nature and relationships, the highest possible good must result. Truthfulness seeks the *good* as an end and *truth* as a means to secure this end. It wills the good and that it shall be secured only by means of truth. It wills truth in the end and truth in the means. The end is *truly* valuable and chosen for that reason. And truth is the only appropriate means.

Truthfulness of heart produces a state in the emotions which we call the love of truth. It is a feeling of pleasure that spontaneously arises in the emotions of one whose heart is truthful in contemplating truth. This *feeling* is not virtue; it is rather a part of the reward of truthfulness of heart.

Truthfulness as a phenomenon of the will is also often called a love of the truth. It is a willing in accordance with objective truth. This is virtue, and is an attribute of benevolence. Truth as an attribute of the divine benevolence is the ground of confidence in God as a moral governor. Both the physical and moral law of the universe manifest this and are instances and illustrations of the truthfulness of God. Falsehood, in the sense of lying, is naturally regarded by a moral agent with disapproval, disgust and abhorrence. Truth is as necessarily regarded by him with approval, and if the will is benevolent, with pleasure. We necessarily take pleasure in contemplating objective truth as we think about it in our consciousness. We also take pleasure in the perception and contemplation of truthfulness, in the concrete realization of the idea of truth. Truthfulness is moral beauty. We are pleased with it just as we are with natural beauty by a law of necessity, when the necessary conditions are fulfilled.

This attribute of benevolence will no more resort to falsehood as a means of promoting good than it can contradict or deny itself. The intelligence affirms that the highest ultimate good can be secured only by a strict adherence to truth, for this adherence is a demand of the intelligence, and the mind cannot be satisfied with anything else. Indeed, to suppose the contrary is to suppose a contradiction. It is the same absurdity as to suppose that the highest good could be secured only by the violation and setting aside of the nature and relations of things.

Since the intelligence affirms this unalterable relation of truth to the highest ultimate good, benevolence or that attribute of benevolence which we call truthfulness or love of the truth can no more consent to falsehood than it can consent to relinquish the highest good of being as an end. And in no case, then, does or can a moral agent violate truth unless he has for the time being at least become selfish and prefers a present gratification to the highest ultimate good of being.

Therefore, every resort to falsehood, every pious fraud, falsely so called, is not only a deception but a real instance of selfishness. A moral agent cannot lie for God—that is, he cannot tell a sinful falsehood, thinking and intending thereby to please God. He knows by intuition that God cannot be pleased or truly served by resorting to lying. There is a great difference between concealing or withholding the truth for benevolent purposes and telling a willful falsehood.

For example, an innocent, persecuted and pursued man has taken shelter from one who pursued him to kill him under my roof. His pursuer comes and inquires after him. I am not under obligation to declare to him that he is in my house. I may, and indeed ought to, withhold the truth in this instance, for the wretch has no right to know it. The public and highest good demands that he should not know it. He only desires to know it for selfish and bloody purposes. But in this case I should not feel free to state a known falsehood. I could not think that this would ultimately be conducive to the highest good. The person might go away deceived or under the impression that his victim was not there. But he could not accuse me of telling him a lie. He might have drawn his own inference from my refusing to give the desired information. But even to secure my own life or the life of my friend, I am not at liberty to tell a lie. I may pray to be rescued, as God rescued Daniel in the lions' den.

If it is said that lying implies telling a falsehood for selfish purposes, and that therefore it is not lying to tell a falsehood for benevolent purposes, I reply that our nature is such that we can no more state a willful falsehood with a benevolent intention than we can commit a sin with a benevolent intention. We necessarily regard falsehood as inconsistent with the highest good of being, just as we regard sin as inconsistent with the highest good of being, or just as we regard holiness and truthfulness as the indispensable conditions of the highest good of being. The correlation of the will and the intelligence forbids that we ever fall into the mistake of thinking that willful falsehood is or can be the means or conditions of the highest good.

Universal truthfulness, then, will always characterize a truly benevolent man. While he is truly benevolent he is, he must be, faithful and truthful. So far as his knowledge goes, his statements may be depended upon with as much safety as the statements of an angel, or as the statements of God himself. Truthfulness is necessarily an attribute of benevolence. No liar has or can have a particle of virtue or benevolence in him.

The opposite of this is *falsehood* or *lying* which is another attribute of selfishness. Falsehood also may be objective or subjective. Objective falsehood is that which stands opposed to truth. Subjective falsehood is a heart conformed to error and to objective falsehood. Subjective falsehood is a state of mind or an attribute of selfishness. It is an attitude of the will that resists truth and embraces error and lies. This is always an attribute of selfishness.

Selfishness is the choice of an end opposed to all truth, and cannot but try to accomplish that end in conformity with error or falsehood instead of truth. If at any time it seizes upon objective truth, as it often does, it is with a false intention. It is with an intention at war with the truth, the nature, and the relationships of things.

If any sinner at any time and under any circumstances tells the truth, it is for a selfish reason. It is to achieve a false end. He has a lie in his heart and a lie in his right hand. He stands upon falsehood. He lives for it, and if he does not uniformly and openly falsify the truth, it is because objective truth is consistent with subjective falsehood. His heart is totally false. It has embraced and sold itself to the greatest lie in the universe. The selfish man has virtually proclaimed that his good is the supreme good, that there is no other good or rights but his own, that all are bound to serve him, and that all interests are to yield to his. Now all this, as I have said, is the greatest falsehood that ever was or can be. Yet this is the solemn practical declaration of every sinner. His selfish choice affirms that God has no rights, that God ought not to be loved and obeyed, that God has no right to govern the universe, but that God and all beings ought to obey and serve the sinner. Can there be a greater or more shameless falsehood than all this? And shall such a person pretend to regard the truth? Never! The very pretense is only an instance and an illustration of the truth that falsehood is an essential element of his character.

If every sinner on earth does not openly and at all times falsify the truth, it is not because of the truthfulness of his heart, but for some purely selfish reason. This must be. His heart is utterly false. It is impossible that, remaining a sinner, he should have any true regard for truth. He is a liar in his heart. This is an essential and eternal attribute of his character. It is true that his intelligence condemns falsehood and justifies truth, and that oftentimes through the intelligence a deep impression is felt in his emotions in favor of the truth. But if the heart is unchanged, it holds on to lies, and perseveres in the practical proclamation of the greatest lies in the universe— that is, that God ought not to be trusted; that Christ is not worthy of confidence; that one's own interest is the supreme good; and that all interests ought to be accounted of less value than one's own.

FOR REFLECTION

I will never tell a lie as a means for achieving any good purpose, and I will trust in the power of a supernatural God to defend me at all times as I stand and proclaim the truth for good and loving reasons.

14

LOVE IS PATIENT

"Love is patient, love is kind. It does not envy, it does not boast, it is not proud" (1 Cor. 13:4).

Patience is another attribute of love. Patience is frequently used to express a phenomenon of the emotions. When used this way, it designates a calm and unruffled state of the feelings under circumstances that tend to excite anger or impatience of feeling. The calmness of the emotions, or patience as a phenomenon of the emotions, is purely an involuntary state of mind, and although it is a pleasing and amiable manifestation, yet it is not properly virtue. It may be, and often is an effect of patience as a phenomenon of the will, and therefore an effect of virtue. But it is not itself virtue. This amiable temper may and often does proceed from the natural temperament, from circumstances, and from habits.

Patience as a virtue must be a volitional state of mind. It must be an attribute of love or benevolence, for all virtue, as we have seen and as the Bible teaches, is but a manifestation of love or benevolence. The term *upomone* in Greek, so often rendered *patience* in the New Testament, means perseverance under trials, persistence, bearing up under afflictions or privations, and steadfastness of purpose in spite of obstacles. The word may be used in a good or in a bad sense. Thus a selfish person may perseveringly pursue his end and may bear up under much opposition to his course. This is patience as an attribute of selfishness, and patience in a bad sense of the term.

Patience in the good sense, or in the sense in which I am considering it, is an attribute of benevolence. It is constancy of intention, a stability, a bearing up under trials, afflictions, crosses, persecutions or discouragements. This must be an attribute of benevolence. Whenever patience ceases, when it holds out no longer, when discouragement prevails and the will relinquishes its end, benevolence ceases of course.

Patience as a phenomenon of the will leads to patience as a phenomenon of the sensibility. That is, stability and steadfastness of intention naturally tend to keep down and quiet impatience of temper. Since, however, the states of the emotions are not directly under the control of the will, there may be irritable or impatient feelings when the heart remains steadfast. Facts or falsehoods may be suggested to the mind that may in spite of the will produce a ruffling of the emotions even when the heart remains patient. The *only* way in which a temptation (for it is only a temptation while the will abides firm to its purpose) of this kind can be disposed of is by diverting the attention from the subject that creates the disturbance in the emotions.

Although the will controls the feelings by a law of necessity, yet, as it does not do so directly but indirectly, it may and often does happen that feelings corresponding to the state of the will do not always exist in the emotional realm. For a time, emotions may exist which are opposite the state of the will. From this source arises many and indeed most of our temptations. We could never be properly tried or tempted at all if the feelings must always by a law of necessity correspond with the state of the will. Sin is choosing to gratify our feelings or natural impulses in opposition to the law of our reason. But if these desires and impulses could never exist in opposition to the law of the reason, and consequently in opposition to a present holy choice, then a holy being could not be tempted. He could have no motive or occasion to sin.

If Eve never could have had feelings of desire in opposition to her will, she never could have desired the forbidden fruit, and of course could not have sinned. I wish to state distinctly that the choice of the will does not necessarily so control the feelings, desires or emotions. These are sometimes strongly excited by Satan or by circumstances in opposition to the will, and thus become powerful temptations to seek their gratification instead of seeking the highest good of being. Feelings whose gratification would be opposed to every attribute of benevolence may at times coexist with benevolence, and be a temptation to selfishness; but opposing acts of the will cannot coexist with benevolence. All that can be truly said is that since the will has an indirect control of the feelings, desires, appetites, passions, etc., it can suppress any class of feelings when they arise by diverting the attention from their causes or by concentrating on the truth and facts which will calm or change the state of the emotions.

Irritable feelings, or what is commonly called impatience, may be directly caused by ill health, irritable nerves, and by many things over which the will has no control. But this is not impatience in the sense of sin. If these feelings are not allowed to influence the will; if the will abides in patience; if such feelings are not cherished and are not allowed to shake the integrity of the will; they are not sin. That is, they can be no sin in themselves. They are only temptations. If they are allowed to control the will, to break forth in words and actions, then there is sin; the sin does not consist in the feelings, but in the consent of the will to gratify them. Thus, the Apostle says, "Be angry and sin not; let not the sun go down upon your wrath" (Eph. 4:26). That is, if anger arises in the feelings, do not sin by allowing it to control your will. Do not cherish the feeling and let the sun go down upon it. When it is cherished, the will consents and broods over the cause of it; this is sin. But if it is not cherished, it is not sin.

It is a universal truth that the outward actions will correspond with the states and actions of the will, provided the integrity of the nerves of voluntary motion are preserved, and no opposing force of greater power than that of my volitions are opposed to them. But it is not true to say that feelings and desires cannot exist contrary to the states or decisions of my will. If this were a universal truth, temptation, as I have said, could not exist.

The outward actions will always be in accord with the will; the feelings, generally. Feelings corresponding to the choice of the will, will be the rule, and opposing feelings the exception. But these exceptions may and do exist in perfectly holy beings. They existed in Eve before she consented to sin, and had she resisted them, she would not have sinned. They doubtless existed in Jesus Christ or He could not have been tempted in all points like as we are.

If there are no desires or impulses of the emotions contrary to the state of the will, then temptation could not exist. The desire or impulse must appear on the field of consciousness before it is a motive to action, and of course before it is a temptation to self-indulgence. Just as certainly then as a holy being may be tempted and not sin, it is equally certain that emotions of any kind or of any strength may exist in the feeling realm without sin. If they are not indulged, if the will does not consent to them and to their indulgence or gratification, the soul is not the less but all the more virtuous for their presence.

Patience as a phenomenon of the will must strengthen and gird itself under such circumstances so that patience of will may be, and if it exists at all, must be, in exact proportion to the *impatience* of the emotions. The more feeling of impatience there is, the more patience of will there must be, or virtue will cease altogether. It is, therefore, not always true that virtue is the strongest when the emotions are the most calm, placid and patient. When Christ passed through His greatest conflicts, His virtue as a man was undoubtedly very intense. When Jesus faced His agony in the garden, the agony of His emotions was so great that He sweat as it were great drops of blood. This, He says, was the hour of the Prince of Darkness. This was His great trial. But did He sin? No, indeed! But why? Was He calm and placid as a summer's evening? He was as far from it as possible.

Patience as an attribute of benevolence does not consist in placid feeling, but in perseverance under trials and states of the emotions that tend to selfishness. This is benevolence viewed in a certain aspect. It is benevolence under circumstances of discouragement, trial or temptation. "This is the patience of the saints."

I would also like to point out that the steadfastness of the heart tends so strongly to secure patience that if an opposite state of the emotions is more than of momentary duration, there is strong presumption that the heart is not steadfast in love. The first risings of it will produce an immediate effort to suppress it. If it continues, this is evidence that the attention is allowed to dwell upon the cause of it. This shows that the will is in some sense indulging it.

If it influences the will enough to manifest itself in impatient words and actions, there must be a yielding of the will. Patience as an attribute of benevolence is overcome. If the emotions were perfectly and directly under the control of the will, the least degree of impatience would imply sin. Momentary impatience of feeling where it does not at all influence the will, and when it is not at all indulged, is not sure evidence of a sinful state of the will. It should always be kept in mind that neither patience nor impatience in the form of mere feeling existing for any length of time and in any degree is in itself either holy on the one hand or sinful on the other. All that can be said of these states of the emotions is that as a general thing they indicate the attitude of the will. When the will continues steadfast in its patience for a long time, it produces a great calmness of temper and great patience of feeling. This becomes a law of the emotions insomuch that very advanced saints may and doubtless do experience the most entire patience of feeling for many years. This does not constitute their holiness, but is a sweet fruit of it. It is to be regarded rather in the light of a reward of holiness than of holiness itself.

Long-suffering is an attribute of benevolence that is hardly distinguishable from meekness or forbearance. It seems to be an intense form of forbearance; or it is forbearance exercised long and under great suffering from persecution and unreasonable opposition. God's forbearance is drawn out to long-suffering. Christ's forbearance also was and often is today put to the severest trial, and is drawn out to the most touching long-suffering. This is an intense state or form of benevolence when it is most sorely tried and as it were put upon the rack.

The prophets and Christ, the apostles and martyrs, and the

primitive saints and many in different ages of the church have set forth a glorious demonstration and illustration of this sweet attribute of love. But for the existence of sin, however, it is probable and perhaps certain that no being but God could have had an idea of its existence. The same, no doubt, may be said of many of the attributes of divine love. God has undoubtedly intended to strongly exhibit this attribute in himself and in all His saints and angels. The introduction of sin, which was excuseless and abominable, has given occasion for a most thorough development and a most touching manifestation of this attribute of love. It is a sweet, heavenly attribute, the exact opposite of the spirit and maxims of this world. It is the very contrast of the law and the spirit of honor as it appears in this world. The law of honor says, "If you receive an injury or an insult, resent it and retaliate." The gentle spirit says, "If you receive many insults and injuries, do not resent them nor retaliate, but bear and forbear even to long-suffering."

The opposite of this is *impatience* which is an attribute of selfishness.

Impatience expresses both a state of the emotions and the will. Impatience is a resistance of providence. When this term is used to express a state of the emotions, it means fretfulness, ill temper, anger in the form of emotion. It is an unsubmissive and rebellious state of feeling in regard to those trials that occur under the administration of the providential government of God.

When the term is used to express a state of the will, it means an attribute of resistance to God's providential dispensations. Selfishness has no faith in God, no confidence in His wisdom and goodness, and being set upon self-gratification is continually exposed to disappointment. God is infinitely wise and benevolent. He also exercises a universal providence. He is conducting everything with reference to the greatest good of the whole universe. He will often interfere with the selfish projects of those who are pursuing an opposite end to that which He pursues. They will, of course, be subject to almost continual disappointment under such a providence because He will make use of all events in accordance with a design which is always at war with their own selfish end. The schemes of selfishness under such a government will frequently be blown to the winds, and a selfish person will be the subject of incessant crosses, vexations and trials. Self-will will always be impatient under a benevolent government. Selfishness would of course have everything so disposed so as to favor self-interest and self-gratification. But infinite wisdom and benevolence cannot accommodate itself to this state of mind. The result must be a constant rasping and collision between the selfish soul and the providence of God. Selfishness must cease to be selfishness before it can be otherwise.

A selfish state of will must, of course, not only resist crosses and disappointments, but must also produce a feverish and fretful state of feeling in relationship to the everyday trials of life. Nothing but deep sympathy with God and that confidence in His wisdom and goodness and universal providence that annihilates self-will and produces universal and unqualified submission to Him can prevent impatience. Impatience is always a form of selfishness. It is resistance to God. It is self-will. Selfishness must be gratified or it will always be displeased. It should always be understood that when trials produce impatience of heart, the will is in a selfish attitude. The trials of this life are designed to develop a submissive, confiding and patient state of mind. A selfish spirit is represented in the Bible as being, under the providence of God, like a bullock unaccustomed to the yoke, stubborn, self-willed, impatient and rebellious.

When selfishness or self-will is subdued and benevolence is practiced, we are in a state where we are apt not to feel disappointments, trials and crosses. Having no way or will of our own about anything, and having deep sympathy with and confidence in God, we cannot be disappointed in any such sense as to vex our spirit and break the peace of our soul.

The fact is that selfishness must be abandoned before we can experience peace. "The wicked are like the troubled sea when it can not rest, whose waters cast up mire and dirt. There is no peace to the wicked, saith my God" (Isa. 57:20–21). This is an impressive figure to represent the continually agitated state in which a selfish mind must be under a perfectly benevolent providence. Selfishness demands partiality in providence that will favor self. But benevolence will not bend to its inclinations. This must produce resistance and fretting, or selfishness must be abandoned. Let it be remembered that impatience is an attribute of selfishness and will always be developed under crosses and trials.

Selfishness will, of course, be patient while providence favors its schemes, but when crosses come, then the peace of the soul is broken.

FOR REFLECTION

I will be patient and praise God for everything, since by His providence He will always overrule evil for good in the highest interests of His Kingdom.

15

LOVE IS MEEK

"Blessed are the meek, for they will inherit the earth" (Matt. 5:5).

Meekness is another attribute of love, and is considered a virtue when it is a phenomenon of the will. The term is also used to express a state of the emotions. When it is used to designate a phenomenon of the feelings, it is nearly synonymous with patience: it means a sweet and forbearing temper under provocation. As a phenomenon of the will and as an attribute of benevolence, it represents a state of will which is the opposite of resistance to injury or retaliation. It is properly and strictly forbearance under injurious treatment.

Meekness is certainly an attribute of God, as our existence and our being out of hell plainly demonstrates. Christ said of himself that He was "meek and lowly in heart," and surely this was no vain boast. How admirably and how continuously did this attribute of His love manifest itself! The fifty-third chapter of Isaiah is a prophecy portraying this attribute in a most touching light. Indeed, scarcely any feature of the character of God and of Christ is more strikingly portrayed than this.

Meekness must be an attribute of benevolence. Benevolence is goodwill to all beings. We are naturally forbearing toward those whose good we honestly and diligently seek. If our hearts are set upon doing them good, we will naturally exercise great forbearance toward them. God has greatly commended His forbearance to us in that while we were yet His enemies, He forbore to punish us, and gave His Son to die for us. Forbearance is a sweet and amiable attribute. How impressively it displayed itself in the hall of Pilate and on the cross. "As a lamb for the slaughter and as a sheep before its shearers is dumb, so he opened not his mouth" (Isa. 53:7).

Meekness has in this world abundant opportunity to develop and display itself through the saints. There are daily occasions for the exercise of this form of virtue. In fact, all the attributes of benevolence are called into frequent exercise in this school of discipline. This truly is a noble world in which to train God's children to develop and strengthen every aspect of holiness. This attribute must always appear where benevolence exists, wherever there is an occasion to practice it.

It is delightful to contemplate the perfection and glory of that love that constitutes obedience to the law of God. As occasions arise, we see love developing one attribute after another, and there may be many of its attributes and aspects or variations of which we have as yet no idea whatsoever. Circumstances will call them into exercise. It is probable, if not certain, that the attributes of benevolence were very imperfectly known in heaven previous to the existence of sin in the universe, and that but for sin many of these attributes would never have been manifested in actual practice. But the existence of sin, great as the evil is, has afforded an opportunity for benevolence to manifest its beautiful phases and to develop its attributes in a most enchanting manner. Thus the divine economy of benevolence brings good out of great evil.

A hasty and unforbearing spirit is always demonstrative evidence of a lack of benevolence or true religion. Meekness is and must be a peculiar characteristic of the saints in this world where so much provocation exists. Christ frequently and strongly enforced the obligation of forbearance. "But I say unto you that ye resist not evil; but whosoever shall smite thee on thy right cheek, turn to him the other also. And if any man will sue thee at the law and take away thy coat, let him have thy cloak also. And whosoever shall compel thee to go a mile, go with him twain" (Matt. 5:39). How beautiful!

The opposite of this is *pride* which is another attribute of selfishness.

Pride is a disposition to exalt self above others, to get out of one's proper place in the scale of being, and to climb up over the heads of our equals or superiors. Pride is a type of injustice on the one hand, and is nearly allied to ambition on the other. It is not a term of so extensive meaning as either injustice or ambition. It is closely related to each of them, but is not identical with either. Pride is a kind of self-praise, self-worship, self-flattery, self-adoration, a spirit of self-consequence, of self-importance. It is an exalting not merely one's interest, but one's person above others, and above God and above all other beings.

A proud being supremely regards himself. He worships and can worship no one but self. He does not, and remaining selfish he cannot, practically admit that there is anyone so good and worthy as himself. He aims at conferring supreme favor upon himself, and virtually admits no claim of any being in the universe to any good or interest that will interfere with his own. He can stoop to give preference to the interest, the reputation, the authority of no one, no not of God himself. His practical language is, "Who is Jehovah that *I* should be humble." Pride is an essential aspect or attribute of selfishness. Sinners are represented in the Bible as proud, as "flattering themselves in their own eyes."

Pride is not a vice distinct from selfishness, but is only a variation of selfishness. Selfishness is the root or stock from which every form of sin sprouts. Selfishness has hardly been regarded by many as a vice, much less as constituting the whole of vice; consequently, when selfishness has been most apparent, it has been supposed and assumed that there might be along with it many forms of virtue. It is for this reason that I find it extremely important to clearly define what are the essential elements of selfishness. It has been supposed that selfishness might exist in any heart without implying every form of sin; that a person might be selfish and yet not proud. In short, it has been overlooked that where selfishness exists, every form of sin must exist. Where there is one form of selfishness manifested, it is a breach of every commandment of God and implies, in fact, the real existence of every possible form of sin and abomination in the heart. My goal is to pursue this course of instruction so far and no further than will fully develop in your minds the great truth that where selfishness is, there must be in a state either of development or of undevelopment every form of sin that exists in earth or hell; that all sin is a unit, and where some form of selfishness is, all sin must be.

The only reason that pride as a form of selfishness does not appear in all sinners in the most disgusting forms is only that their natural temperament and providential circumstances are such as to give a more prominent development to some other attribute of selfishness. It is important to remark that where any one form of unqualified sin exists, there selfishness must exist, and there, of course, every form of sin must exist, at least in embryo, waiting only for providential circumstances to develop it. When therefore you see any form of sin, know assuredly that the root of selfishness is there, and expect nothing else, if selfishness continues, than to see developed, one after one, every form of sin as the providence of God shall present the occasion. Selfishness is a volcano, sometimes smothered, but which must have vent. The providence of God cannot but present occasions upon which its lava-tides will burst forth and carry desolation before them.

That all these forms of sin exist has been known and admitted. But it does not appear to me that the philosophy of sin has been properly considered by many. It is important that we should get at the fundamental or universal form of sin, that form which includes and implies all others, or more properly, which constitutes the whole of sin. Such is selfishness. "Let it be written with the point of a diamond and engraved in the rock forever" that it may be known that where selfishness exists, there every precept of the law is violated, there is the whole of sin. Its guilt and punishment must depend upon the light with which the selfish mind is surrounded. But sin, the whole of sin, is there.

FOR REFLECTION

I will count others better than myself, and I will intercede in prayer for and speak the truth in love to those who try my patience with their rejection of the Gospel of Jesus Christ and me personally.

16

LOVE IS HUMBLE

"Blessed are the poor in spirit, for theirs is the kingdom of heaven" (Matt. 5:3).

Humility is another aspect of the attribute of love. Humility often seems to be used to express a sense of unworthiness, of guilt, of ignorance, and of nothingness, to express a feeling of deserving punishment. Sometimes it is used in common language to express a state of the intelligence; it seems to indicate a clear perception of our guilt. When used to mean a state of the emotions, it represents those feelings of shame and unworthiness, of ignorance and or nothingness, of which people are so conscious when they have been enlightened by the Holy Spirit with respect to their true character.

As a phenomenon of the will, and as an attribute of love, it is a *willingness to be known and appreciated according to our real character.* Humility as a phenomenon either of the emotions or of the intelligence may coexist with great pride of heart. Pride is a disposition to exalt self, to get above others, to hide our defects and to pass for more than we are. Deep conviction of sin and deep feelings of shame, of ignorance, and of deserving of hell may coexist with a *great unwillingness* to confess and be known just as we are, and to be appreciated just according to what our real character has been and is. There is no virtue in such humility.

Considered as a virtue, humility is the consent of the will

to be known, to confess, and to take its proper place in the scale of being. It is that peculiarity of love that wills the good of being so disinterestedly as to will to pass for no other than we really are. This is an honest, sweet and amiable feature of love. It must, perhaps, be peculiar to those who have sinned. It is only love acting under or in a certain relationship or set of circumstances. It would under the same circumstances develop and manifest itself in all truly benevolent minds. This attribute will make confession of sin to God and man natural, even a luxury. It is easy to see that if it weren't for this attribute, the saints could not be happy in heaven. God has promised to bring into judgment every work and every secret thing whether it be good or evil. Now, while pride exists, it would greatly pain the soul to have all its character known. Unless this attribute really belongs to the saints, they would be ashamed at the judgment and filled with confusion even in heaven itself. But this sweet attribute will protect them against that shame and confusion of face that would otherwise render heaven itself a hell to them. They will be perfectly willing and happy to be known and estimated according to their characters.

This attribute will produce in all the saints on earth that confession of faults one to another which is so often recommended in the Bible. By this it is not intended that Christians always think it wise and necessary to make confession of all their secret sins to others, only to those whom they have injured and to all to whom benevolence demands that they should confess. One who possesses this attribute is guarded against spiritual pride and ambition to get above others. Humility is a modest and unassuming state of mind.

Egotism, the opposite of humility, is another attribute of selfishness. When properly considered, egotism is not actually talking about and praising oneself, but rather that disposition of mind that manifests itself in self-praise. Parrots talk almost exclusively of themselves, and yet we do not accuse them of egotism nor feel the least disgust toward them on that account.

Moral agents may be under circumstances that make it necessary to speak much of themselves. God's character and relations are such and the ignorance of men so great that it is necessary for Him to reveal himself to them, and consequently to speak to them very much about himself. The same is true of Christ. Christ's principal goal was to make the world acquainted with himself and with the nature and design of His mission. Of course He spoke much of himself. But who ever thought of accusing either the Father or the Son of egotism!

The fact is that real egotism is a selfish state of the will. It is a selfish disposition. Selfishness is the supreme preference of self, of self-interest, of self-indulgence; of course, this state of mind must manifest egotism. The *heart* is egotistical; therefore, the language and behavior will be, too.

An egotistical state of mind manifests itself in a great variety of ways; not just in self-commendation or praise, but also in selfish aims and actions, exalting self in action as well as in word. An egotistical spirit speaks of itself and its achievements in such a way as to reveal the assumption that self is a very important personage. It demonstrates that self is the end of everything and the great idol before which all ought to bow down and worship. This language is not too strong. The fact is, that selfishness is a virtual setting up of the shameless claim that self is of more importance than God and the whole universe; that self ought to be universally worshiped; that God and all other beings ought to be entirely consecrated to the interests of oneself and to the promotion of its glory. Now, what but the most disgusting egotism can be expected from such a state of mind? This state of mind is essentially and necessarily egotistical. If it does not manifest itself in one way, it will and must in another. The thoughts are upon self; the heart is upon self. Self-flattery is a necessary result, or attribute, of selfishness. A selfish person is always a self-flatterer, a self-deceiver, and a self-devotee. This must be.

Self may speak very sparingly of self for the reason that it thinks *too* much of self to willingly incur the charge of egotism. A person may have a spirit too egotistical to speak out, and may reveal his superlative disposition to be praised by a studied abstinence from self-condemnation. He may speak of himself in the most reproachful and self-abasing terms in the spirit of supreme egotism to prove his humility and the deep self-knowledge which he possesses. But a spirit of self-deification, which selfishness always is, if it does not manifest itself in words, must and will in deeds. The great and supreme importance of self is assumed by the heart, and in some way will manifest itself. It may, and often does, put on the garb of the utmost self-abasement. It stoops to conquer, to gain universal praise, and appear to be most empty of self.

But this is only a refined egotism. It is only saying, "Come see my perfect humility and self-emptiness." Indeed there are myriads of ways in which an egotistical spirit manifests itself, and so subtle and refined are many of them that they resemble Satan robed in the stolen garments of an angel of light.

An egotistical spirit often manifests itself in self-consequential airs, and by thrusting self into the best seat at a table, in a railroad car, or into the best stateroom in a ship. In short, it manifests in action what it is apt to manifest in word, that is, a sense of supreme self-importance.

I said that the mere fact of speaking of self is not of itself proof of an egotistical spirit. The thing to be regarded is the manner and manifest intention or purpose of speaking of self. A benevolent person may speak much of self because it may be important to others that he should do so, on account of his relationships. When the intention is for the benefit of others and the glory of God, it is as far as possible from the spirit of egotism. A benevolent man might speak of himself just as he would of others. He has merged his interests in, or rather identified them with, the interests of others and, of course, would naturally treat others and speak of them as much as he treats and speaks of himself. If he sees and censures the conduct of others, and has ever been guilty of the same, he will censure his own depravity quite as severely as he does the same thing in others. If he commends the virtues of others, it is but for the glory of God, and for the very same reason he might speak of virtues of which he is conscious in himself, that God may have glory. A perfectly simple-hearted and guileless state of mind might naturally manifest itself in this manner. An egotistical spirit in another might, and doubtless would, lead him to misunderstand such openheartedness and transparency of character. There would be, nevertheless, a radical difference in the spirit with which two such people would speak either of their own faults or virtues.

FOR REFLECTION

I will walk humbly before God and others, because I know that I along with all people have sinned. I know that everyone who is saved is saved only by grace through faith, so no one can boast except in what the Lord has done. When it is necessary to commend myself to others, I will do so only to promote the glory of God and to further His Kingdom. I will practice counting others better than myself.

17

LOVE IS SELF-DENYING

"Jesus answered, 'If you want to be perfect, go, sell your possessions and give to the poor, and you will have treasure in heaven. Then come, follow me' " (Matt. 19:21).

Self-denial is another attribute of love. If we love any being better than ourselves, of course we deny ourselves when our own interests come in competition with his. Love is goodwill. If I will good to others more than to myself, it is absurd to say that I will not deny myself when my own inclinations conflict with theirs.

Now the love required by the law of God which we have repeatedly seen is goodwill, or willing the highest good of being for its own sake or as an end.

Since the interests of self are not at all regarded because they belong to self, but only according to their relative value, it must be certain that self-denial for the sake of promoting the higher interests of God and of the universe is and must be a characteristic or attribute of love.

The very idea of disinterested benevolence (and there is no other true benevolence) implies the abandonment of the spirit of self-seeking or of selfishness. It is impossible to become benevolent without ceasing to be selfish. In other words, perfect self-denial is implied in beginning to be benevolent. Self-indulgence ceases when benevolence begins. This must be. Benevolence is the consecration of our powers to the highest good of being in general as an end. This is utterly inconsistent with consecration to self-interest or self-gratification. Selfishness makes *good to self the end or goal of every choice*. Benevolence makes *good to being in general the end or goal of every choice*. Benevolence, then, implies complete self-denial. That is, it implies that nothing is chosen merely because it belongs to self, but only because of and in proportion to its relative value.

I said there was no true benevolence but disinterested benevolence; no true love but disinterested love. There is such a thing as interested love or benevolence. That is, the good of others is willed, though not as an end or for its intrinsic value to them, but as a means of our own happiness or because of its relative value to us. Thus a person might will the good of his family or of his neighborhood or of his country or of anybody or anything that sustained such relationships to his own self as to involve his own interests. When the ultimate reason of his willing good to others is that his own good may be promoted, this is selfishness. It is making good to self his end or purpose for living. This a sinner may do toward God, toward the church, and toward the interests of religion in general. Such self-seeking is what I call *interested* benevolence. It is willing good as an end only to self, and to all others only as a means of promoting our own good.

When the will is governed by feeling in willing the good of others, this is only the spirit of self-indulgence, and is only interested benevolence. For example, the feeling of compassion is strongly stirred by the presence of misery. The feeling is intense and creates, like all the feelings, a strong impulse or motive to the will to consent to its gratification. For the time being, this impulse is stronger than the feeling of greed or any other feeling. I yield to it and give all the money I have to relieve the sufferer. I even take my clothes off my back and give them to him. Now in this case, I am just as selfish as if I had sold my clothes to gratify my appetite for liquor. The gratification of my feelings was my goal. This is one of the most misleading and delusive forms of selfishness.

When one makes his own salvation the goal of prayer, of almsgiving, and of all his religious duties, this is only selfishness and not true religion, however much the person may abound in them. This is only interested benevolence or benevolence to self.

From the very nature of true benevolence, it is impossible that every interest should not be regarded according to its relative value. When I recognize another interest to be more valuable in itself or of more value to God and the universe than my own, and that by denying myself I can promote it, it is certain, if I am benevolent, that I will do it. I cannot fail to do it without failing to be benevolent. Two things in this case must be understood by the mind:

1. That the interest is either intrinsically or relatively more valuable than my own;

2. That by denying myself I can promote or secure a greater good to being than I sacrifice of my own. When these two conditions are fulfilled, it is impossible to remain benevolent unless I deny myself and seek the higher good.

Benevolence is an *honest and disinterested* consecration of the whole being to the highest good of God and of the universe. The benevolent person will, therefore, and must, honestly weigh each interest as it is perceived in the balance of his own best judgment, and will always give the preference to the higher interest, provided he believes that he can by endeavor and by self-denial secure it.

That self-denial is an attribute of the divine love is manifested in a glorious and moving way in the gift of God's Son to die for us. The attribute of self-denial was also clearly manifested by Christ in denying himself and taking up His cross and suffering for His enemies. Observe it was not for friends that Christ gave himself. It was not for unfortunate or innocent sufferers that God gave His Son or for whom He gave himself. It was for enemies. It was not that He might make slaves of them that He gave His Son, nor from any selfish consideration whatsoever, but because He foresaw that by making this sacrifice himself, He could ensure to the universe a greater good than He should sacrifice. It was this attribute of benevolence that caused Him to give His Son to suffer so much. It was disinterested benevolence alone that led Him to deny himself for the sake of a greater good to the universe. Take particular notice that this sacrifice would not have been made unless it had been regarded by God as the lesser of two evils. That is, the sufferings of Christ, great and overwhelming as they were, were considered as an evil of less magnitude than the eternal sufferings of sinners. This induced Him to make the sacrifice even for His enemies. It mattered not whether for friends or for enemies, if in so doing He could by making a lesser sacrifice ensure a greater good to them. In a later chapter I will speak more on this topic when I consider love as being economical.

You must understand that a self-indulgent spirit is never and can never be consistent with benevolence. No form of self-indulgence, properly so called, can exist where true benevolence exists. The fact is, self-denial must be and universally exists wherever benevolence reigns. Christ has expressly made wholehearted self-denial a condition of discipleship, which is the same as affirming that it is an essential attribute of holiness, or love. There can be no beginning of true virtue without self-denial.

Much that passes for self-denial is only a misleading form of self-indulgence. The penances and self-mortifications, as they are falsely called, of the superstitious, are nothing but manifestations of a self-indulgent spirit after all. A priest abstains from marriage to obtain the honor, benefits and the influence of the priestly office here, and eternal glory hereafter.

A nun takes the veil and a monk encloses himself in a monastery. A hermit forsakes human society, and shuts himself up in a cave. A devotee makes a pilgrimage to Mecca, and a martyr goes to the stake. Now if these things are done with an ultimate reference to their own personal glory and happiness, although apparently instances of great self-denial, yet they are in fact only a spirit of self-indulgence and self-seeking. They are only following the strongest desire. They are instances of making good to self the end.

There are many misconceptions about this subject. For example, it is common for people to deny self in one form for the sake of gratifying self in another form.

In one man greed is the ruling passion. He will labor hard,

rise early, and sit up late and worry, deny himself even the necessities of life for the sake of accumulating wealth. Everyone can see that this is denying self in one form merely to gratify it in another. Yet this man will complain bitterly of the self-indulgent spirit manifested by others, their extravagance and lack of piety.

Another man will deny all his bodily appetites and passions for the sake of a reputation with men. Another will give his children for the sin of his soul. He will sacrifice everything to obtain an eternal inheritance, and be just as selfish as the man who sacrifices to temporal things his soul and all the riches of eternity.

But it should be emphasized that this attribute of benevolence does and must secure the subjugation of all the appetites. It must, either suddenly or gradually, so far subdue and quiet them that their imperious clamor will cease. They will, as it were, be slain either suddenly or gradually so that the emotions will become to a large degree dead to those objects that so often and so easily excited them. It is a law of the emotions, of all the desires and passions, that their indulgence develops and strengthens them and their denial suppresses them. Benevolence is refusing to gratify the emotions and obeying the reason. Therefore, it must be true that this denial of the appetites or desires will greatly suppress them until they become tame and easily denied. While, on the contrary, the indulgence of the appetites and the indulgence of the intelligence and of the conscience will greatly develop them. Thus selfishness tends to dull, while benevolence tends to strengthen the intelligence greatly.

Oppression is another attribute of selfishness. Oppression is the spirit of slaveholding, a disposition to deprive others of their rights for the purpose of contributing to our own interest or gratification. To define it comprehensively: it is a disposition to enslave God and all the universe; to make them all give up their interest and happiness and glory and seek and live for ours. It is a willing that all beings should live to and for *us*; that all interests should bend and be sacrificed to ours. Oppression is a practical denial of all rights but our own, a practical claiming that all beings are ours—our goods or belongings, our property. It is a spirit that aims at making all beings and interests serve us.

Self-interest is the ultimate end or goal of selfishness; and the whole life and activity and aim and effort is to secure this end. The sinner, while he remains such, has absolutely no other end or motive in view. Selfishness or self-gratification in some form or other is the reason for every volition, action or omission. For this end alone he lives. This being his only end, it is evident that oppression is an attribute of his character. Nothing can be more oppressive to the whole universe than for a being to set up his interest as the sole good, and account all other interests as of no value except as they contribute to his own. This is the perfection of oppression, and it matters not what particular course it takes to secure its end. They are all equally oppressive. If he does not seek the good of others for its own sake, but simply as a means of securing his own, it matters not whether he pampers and fattens or starves his slaves, whether he works them hard or lets them lounge, whether he lets them go naked or dresses them in costly attire. All is done for only one ultimate reason—to promote self-interest.

If such a person prays to God, it is because he is unable to command and govern Him by authority, and not out of any true regard to the rights or character or relationships of God. He desires God's services; and because he cannot get them by force, he entreats God in prayer. God's interests and rights are treated as of no value by every sinner in the universe. They care nothing for God except to enslave Him—that is, to make *Him* serve *them* without wages. They have no intention to live to and for Him; they want Him to live to and for them. They regard all people and creatures in just the same manner. If in any instance there is the appearance of a regard to their interest for its own sake, it is only an appearance, not a reality. It is not, and it cannot be, a reality. The assertion that it is anything more than a hypocritical pretense is absurd and contradicts the supposition that he is a sinner or selfish.

There are innumerable misleading forms of oppression that to a superficial observer appear very much like a regard for the real interest of the oppressed for its own sake.

It may be gratifying to the pride, the ambition or to some other *feeling* of a slaveholder to see his slaves well fed, well clad, physically fit, cheerful, contented, attached to their master. For the same reason, he might feed his dog, provide him a warm kennel, and adorn his neck with a brazen collar. He might do the same for his horse and for his swine. But why does he do all this? Self-gratification. God has so molded his nature that it would grieve him to whip his slave or his dog or his horse, or to see them hungry or naked. It would trouble his conscience and endanger his peace and his soul. There often may be the appearance of virtue in a slaveholder and in slaveholding, but it can only be an appearance. If it is true slaveholding, it is and must be oppression; it is and must be selfishness. Can it be that slaveholding is designed to promote the good of the slave for its own sake? But then it could not be slaveholding.

Should a slave be held for his own benefit, or the law of benevolence really demand it, this could no more be the crime of slaveholding and oppression than it is murder or any other crime. It would not be selfishness, but benevolence, and therefore no crime at all—only virtue. But selfishness embodies every element of oppression. Its end—the means and every breath— is but an incessant denial of all rights but self. All *sinners are oppressors* and slaveholders in heart and fact. They practice continual oppression and nothing else. They make God serve them without wages, and they, as He says, "make him to serve with their sins." God, all men, all things and events are, as far as possible, made to serve them without the return of the least disinterested regard to their interests. Disinterested regard! Why, the very term contradicts the supposition that he is a sinner! He has, he can have, in no instance any other than selfish aims in appearing to care for anyone's interest for its own sake.

All *unconverted abolitionists* are slaveholders in heart and so far as possible in outward behavior. There is not one of them who would not enslave every slave in the South and his master too, and all in the North and the whole universe, and God himself as far as he could. Indeed he does, and remaining selfish, he cannot but aim to enslave all beings, to make them as far as possible contribute to his interests and pleasure without the least disinterested regard to their interest in return.

Oppression is an essential attribute of selfishness and always develops itself according to circumstances. When it has power, it uses the chain and the whip. When it has no power, it resorts to other means of securing the services of others without disinterested return. Sometimes oppression supplicates and prays; but this is only because it is regarded as necessary or expedient. It is oppression under whatever form it assumes. It is in fact a denial of all rights but those of self rights, and a practical claiming of God and all beings and events as ours. In reality it is the slave principle universally applied. As a result, all sinners are both slaveholders and slaves; in heart and endeavor they enslave God and all men; and other sinners in heart and endeavor enslave them. Every sinner is endeavoring in heart to gain for himself all good.

FOR REFLECTION

I have chosen to put the good of God and the universe above my own, and I know that this is best for God, the universe and myself. However, I have not made this my goal in life for selfish reasons, to go to heaven or to have financial blessings or happiness. This is my goal in life because of God's great love for me, and because I love Him for all that He is and for all that He is doing in behalf of others. I want to love and serve others, just as He is loving and serving others, too.

18

LOVE IS CONDESCENDING

"Religion that God our Father accepts as pure and faultless is this: to look after orphans and widows in their distress and to keep oneself from being polluted by the world" (James 1:27).

Condescension is another attribute of love. It consists in a willingness to descend to the poor, the ignorant, or the vile for the purpose of securing their good. It is willing the good of those whom providence has placed in any respect below us, together with the means of securing their good, particularly our own stooping, descending, coming down to them for this purpose. It is a peculiar form of self-denial.

God—the Father, the Son, and the Holy Spirit—manifests infinite condescension in efforts to secure the well-being of sinners, even the most vile and degraded. Christ calls this attribute lowliness of heart. God is said to humble himself; that is, to condescend when He beholds the things that are done in heaven. This is true, for every creature is, and must forever be, infinitely below God in every respect. But how much greater must that condescension be that comes down to earth, and even to the lowest and most degraded of earth's inhabitants, for purposes of benevolence. This is a lovely modification of benevolence. It seems to be entirely above the gross conception of infidelity.

Condescension seems to be regarded by most people, and especially by infidels, as a weakness rather than a virtue. Skeptics clothe their imaginary god with attributes, which are, in many respects, the opposite of true virtue. They think it entirely beneath the dignity of God to come down even to notice, much more to interfere with, the concerns of men. But hear the word of the Lord: "Thus saith the High and Lofty One who inhabiteth eternity, whose name is Holy. I dwell in the high and holy place; with him also that is of a contrite and humble spirit, to revive the spirit of the humble and to revive the heart of the contrite ones" (Isa. 57:15). And again, "Thus saith the Lord, the heaven is my throne and the earth is my footstool, where is the house that ye build unto me? and where is the place of my rest? For all those things hath my hand made, and all those things have been, saith the Lord. But to this man will I look even to him that is poor and of a contrite spirit, and trembleth at my word" (Isa. 66:1–2). Thus the Bible represents God as clothed with condescension as with a cloak.

This is manifestly an attribute of benevolence and of true greatness. The natural perfections of God appear all the more wonderful when we consider that He can and does know and contemplate and control not only the highest but the lowest of all His creatures; that He is just as able to attend to every need and to every creature as if this were the only object of attention with Him. So His moral attributes appear all the more lovely and delightful when we consider that His "tender mercies are over all his works," that "not a sparrow falleth to the ground without him"; that He condescends to number the very hairs of the heads of His servants, and that not one of them can fall without Him. When we consider that no creature is too low, too filthy, or too degraded for Him to condescend to, this places His character in a most ravishing light. Benevolence is goodwill to all beings. One of its characteristics, of course, must be condescension to those who are below us. In God this is manifestly infinite. He is infinitely above all creatures. For Him to hold communion with us is infinite condescension.

Condescension is an attribute essentially belonging to benevolence or love in all benevolent beings. With the lowest of moral beings, it may have no other development than in its relationships to cognizant existences below the rank of moral agents, for the reason that there are no moral agents below them to whom they can stoop. God's condescension stoops to all ranks of cognizant existences. This is also true with every benevolent mind, as to all inferiors. It seeks the good of being in general, and never thinks any being too low to have his interests attended to and cared for, according to their relative value. Benevolence cannot possibly retain its own essential nature, and yet be above any degree of condescension that can bring about the greatest good. Benevolence does not, cannot, know anything of the loftiness of spirit that considers it too degrading to stoop anywhere or to any being whose interests need to be and can be promoted by such condescension. Benevolence has its end, and it cannot but seek this, and it does not, cannot, think anything below it that is demanded to secure that end. Oh, the shame, the infinite folly and madness of pride, and every form of selfishness! How infinitely unlike God it is! Christ could condescend to be born in a manger; to be brought up in humble life; to be poorer than the fox of the desert or the fowls of heaven; to associate with fishermen; to mingle with and seek the good of all classes; to be despised in life, and die between two thieves on the cross. His benevolence "endured the cross and despised the shame." He was "meek and lowly in heart." The Lord of heaven and earth is as much more lowly in heart than any of His creatures as He is above them in His infinity. He can stoop to anything but sin. He can stoop infinitely low.

The opposite of condescension is *war*, which is an attribute of selfishness. War is strife, and is opposed to peace and amity. On the very face of selfishness is a declaration of war with all beings. It is setting up self-interest *in opposition* to all other interests. It is an attempt and a deliberate intention to seize upon and subordinate all interests to our own. It is impossible to have anything but perpetual hostility between a selfish being and all benevolent beings. They are mutually and necessarily opposed to each other. The benevolent are seeking the universal good, and the selfish are seeking their own gratification without the least voluntary regard to any interest but that of self. Here is opposition and war of course and of necessity.

But it is no less true that every selfish being is at war with every other selfish being. Each is seeking and fully consecrated to his own interest and denying all rights but his own. Here is and must be war. There is no use in talking of putting away slavery or war from the earth while selfishness is in it, for they both are offshoots of the very nature of selfishness. And every selfish being is an oppressor, a slaveholder, a tyrant, a warrior, a duelist, a pirate, and all that is implied in making war upon all beings. This is no railing accusation, but sober truth. The forms of war and oppression may be modified indefinitely. The bloody sword may be sheathed. The manacle and the lash may be laid aside, and a more refined mode of oppression and war may be carried on; but oppression and war must continue under some form so long as selfishness continues. It is impossible that it should not.

Nor will the more refined and apparently good, and if you please, baptized forms of oppression and war that may succeed those now practiced involve less guilt and be less displeasing to God than the present. No indeed. As light increases and compels selfishness to lay aside the sword and bury the manacle and the whip and profess the religion of Christ, the guilt of selfishness increases every moment. The former manifestation is changed, compelled by increasing light and advancing civilization and Christianization. Oppression and war, although so much changed in form, are not at all abandoned in fact. No, they are only strengthened by increasing light.

Nor can it be told or so much as rationally conjectured whether the more refined modifications of oppression and war that may succeed will, upon the whole, be a real benefit to mankind. Guilt will certainly increase as light increases. Sin abounds and becomes exceeding sinful in proportion to the light of truth poured upon the selfish mind; and whether it is a real good to promote mere outward reform without reforming the heart, who can tell? The fact is, selfishness must be done away with; the ax must be laid to the root of the tree. It is a mistaken zeal that wastes its energies in merely modifying the forms in which selfishness manifests itself in changing the modes of oppression and war and bringing about mere refinements in sin. I cannot during my life respect in myself or in others such efforts. What do they amount to after all, but to whitewash and baptize a sinner and gather about him a delusion deep as death and send him by the shortest way to hell? All such efforts remind me of an affirmation I once heard a preacher make, namely, that "self-righteousness is good so far as it goes, but it is like a coat without sleeves."

Many seem to think that to bring about mere outward reform is a profitable good. But it is no real good unless true virtue and happiness are gained. Unless selfishness is put away, it is no positive good. Whether, then, outward reforms will prove to be the lesser of two evils, who can tell? Do you ask, then, "What shall we do? Shall we do nothing, but let things go on as they are?" I answer, no, by no means. Do, if possible, ten times more than ever to put away these and all the evils that are under the sun. But aim at the annihilation of selfishness, and when you succeed in reforming the heart, the life cannot help but be reformed. Put away selfishness and oppression and war will cease. But engage in bringing about any other reform, and you are but building dams of sand. Selfishness will force a channel for itself; and who can say that its desolations may not be more fearful and calamitous in this new modification than before? Attempting to reform selfishness and teach it better manners is like damming up the waters of the Mississippi. It will only surely overflow its banks and change its channel, and carry devastation and death in its wake. I am aware that many will regard this as a heresy. But God sees not as man sees. Man looks on the outward appearance, but God looks on the heart. God winks at all the wars and filthiness of heathenism as comparatively a light thing when put into the scale against the most refined form of intelligent but heartless Christianity that ever existed.

In conclusion, let it be forever understood that selfishness is at war with all nations and with all beings. It has no element of peace in it any further than all beings and all interests are yielded to the gratification of self. This is its essential, its unalterable nature. This attribute cannot cease while selfishness remains.

All selfish people who are advocates of peace principles are necessarily hypocrites. They say and do not. They preach but do not practice. Peace is on their lips, but war is on their hearts. They proclaim peace and goodwill to men, while under their stolen robe of peace, they conceal their poisoned weapons of war against God and the universe. I am anxious to make the impression and lodge it deep in your inmost hearts, so that you shall always hold, and teach, and regard this as a fundamental truth both of natural and revealed religion, that a selfish person, instead of being a Christian, a man of peace, and a servant of the Prince of Peace, is in heart, character, and spirit a rebel, an enemy, a warrior. He is truly at war with God and all beings.

FOR REFLECTION

I will give my attention to the poor, to the downcast, to those rejected by others, and to those who have little or no self-esteem. I will tell them of God's wonderful condescending love in **our** *behalf, and I will demonstrate this love in practical ways.*

19

LOVE IS HONEST

"Dear children, let us not love with words or tongue, but with actions and in truth" (1 John 3:18).

Honesty or *candor* is another attribute of love. Candor is a disposition to treat every subject with fairness and honesty; to examine and weigh all the evidence in the case and decide according to testimony. It is a state of mind which is the opposite of prejudice. Prejudice is pre-judgment. Pre-judgment is a decision made with only partial information. It is not a mere opinion. It is a committal of the will.

Candor is keeping the intelligence open to conviction. It is that state of the will in which all the light that can be obtained is sought in regards to all questions. Benevolence is an impartial, a disinterested choice of the highest good of being—not of some parts of it—not of self—but of being in general. It inquires not to whom an interest belongs, but what is its intrinsic and relative value, and what is the best means of promoting it. Selfishness is never candid, never honest. That is contrary to its very nature. Benevolence, on the other hand, cannot help but be candid. It seeks to know all truth for the sake of doing it. It has no selfishness, no self-will or self-interest to consult. It is not seeking to please or profit self. It is not seeking the interest of some favorite. No, love is impartial and must be candid.

Always bear in mind that where there is prejudice, benevolence is not present and cannot be. There is not, cannot be, such a thing as honest prejudice. There may be an honest mistake for lack of light, but this is not prejudice. If there is a mistake and it is honest, there will be and must be a readiness to receive light to correct the mistake. But where the will is committed, and there is not candor to receive evidence, there is and there must be selfishness. Few forms of sin are more odious and revolting than prejudice. Candor is an amiable and lovely attribute of benevolence. It is captivating to behold. To see a person, where his own interest is deeply concerned, exhibit entire candor is to witness a charming exhibition of the spirit of the law of love.

FOR RELFECTION

I will honestly evaluate my talents and abilities with respect to using them in the service of God, and I will be open to learning from friends and enemies how I can strengthen my weaknesses, with God's help, for the sake of His Kingdom.

20

LOVE IS STABLE

"And so we know and rely on the love God has for us. God is love. Whoever lives in love lives in God, and God in him. Love is made complete among us so that we will have confidence on the day of judgment, because in this world we are like him. There is no fear in love. But perfect love drives out fear, because fear has to do with punishment. The man who fears is not made perfect in love" (1 John 4:16–18).

Stability is another attribute of love. This love is not a mere feeling or emotion that effervesces for a moment and then cools down and disappears. It is choice, and not a mere volition which accomplishes its object and then rests. Stability is the choice of an end, a supreme end or goal. It is an intelligent choice, the most intelligent choice that can be made. Stability is also considerate choice, a deliberate choice, a reasonable choice which will always commend itself to the highest perceptions and intuitions of the intelligence. It is intelligent and impartial, a universal consecration to an end.

Now stability must be a characteristic of such a choice as this. By stability I do not mean that the choice may not be changed, nor that it never is changed. But when the attributes of the choice are considered, it appears as if stability, as opposed to instability, must be an attribute of this choice. It is a new birth, a new nature, a new creature, a new heart, a new life. These are the representations of Scripture. Are these representations gradually fading away? The beginning of benevolence in the soul is the choice which manifests itself as the death of sin, as a burial, a being planted, a crucifixion of the old man, and many such like things. Are these representations of what we so often see among professed converts to Christ? Not really. The nature of the change itself would seem to be a guarantee of its stability. We might reasonably assume that any other choice would be relinquished sooner than this, that any other state of mind would fail sooner than benevolence. It is vain to reply to this that facts prove the contrary to be true. I answer, what facts? Who can prove them to be facts? Shall we appeal to the apparent facts in the instability of many professors of religion; or shall we appeal to the very nature of the choice and to the Scriptures? To these, doubtless. So far as philosophy can go, we might defy the world to produce an instance of choice which has so many chances for stability. The representations of Scripture are such as I have mentioned above. What then shall we conclude of those effervescing professors of religion, who are soon hot and soon cold, whose religion is a spasm, "whose goodness as the morning cloud and the early dew goeth away"? Why, we must conclude that they have never been rooted in true stability which comes out of the will. We see that they are not dead to sin and to the world. We see that they are not new creatures, that they have not the spirit of Christ, that they do not keep His commandments. What then shall we conclude but this, that they are stony ground Christians.

The opposite of stability is *madness,* which is another attribute of selfishness. Madness is used sometimes to mean anger, sometimes intellectual insanity, and sometimes moral insanity.

I speak of it now in the sense of *moral insanity.*

Moral insanity is not insanity of the intelligence but of the heart. Insanity of the intelligence destroys, for the time being, moral agency and accountability. Moral insanity is a state in which the intellectual powers are not deranged, but the heart refuses to be controlled by the intelligence and acts unreasonably as if the intellect were deranged. Madness or moral insanity is an attribute of selfishness or of a sinful character for the following reasons:

1. The Bible exposes it: "The heart of the sons of men is full of evil, *and madness is in their heart while they live*" (Eccles. 9:3).

2. It has been shown that sinners or selfish people act in every instance directly opposite to right reason. Indeed, nothing can be plainer than the moral insanity of every selfish soul. He prefers to seek his own interest as an end and prefers a straw to a universe. What is so insane is he does this with the certain knowledge that in this way, he can never secure his own highest interest. What an infinitely insane course that must be—first to prefer his own petty gratification to the infinite interests of God and of the universe, and second, to do this with the knowledge that in this way nothing can be ultimately gained even to self, and that if the course is persisted in, it must result in endless evil to self, the very thing which is supremely dreaded! Sin is the greatest mystery, the greatest absurdity, and the greatest contradiction in the universe.

Madness is an essential element or attribute of selfishness. All sinners, without any exception, are and must be mad. Their choice of an end is madness. It is infinitely unreasonable and their pursuit of it results in continual madness. Their treatment of everything that opposes their course is madness. All is infinite madness. This world is a moral bedlam, an insane hospital where sinners are under regimen. If they can be cured, well. If not, they must be confined in the madhouse of the universe for eternity.

The only reason why sinners do not perceive their own and each other's madness is that they are all mad together and their madness is all the same. Hence, they imagine that they are sane, and pronounce Christians mad. This is no wonder. What other conclusion can they come to unless they can discover that they are mad?

But let it not be forgotten that their madness is of the heart, and not of the intellect. It is voluntary and avoidable. If it were unavoidable, it would involve no guilt. But it is a choice made and persisted in in the integrity of their intellectual powers, and therefore they are without excuse.

Sinners are generally assumed to act rationally on many

subjects. But this is an obvious mistake. They do everything for the same ultimate reason and are as wholly irrational in one thing as another. There is nothing in their whole history and life that is not entirely and infinitely unreasonable. The end is mad; the means are mad; all is madness and desperation of spirit. They no doubt appear so both to angels and saints; and were it not so common to see them, their conduct would fill the saints and angels with utter amazement.

Recklessness is another attribute of selfishness which is similar to madness. Recklessness is carelessness, or a state of mind that seeks to gratify self regardless of the consequences. It is a spirit of infatuation, a rushing upon ruin heedless of what may come.

Recklessness is one of the most prominent attributes of selfishness. It is universally prominent and manifest. What can be more manifest and striking and astonishing than the recklessness of every sinner? Self-indulgence is his motto; and the only appearance of consideration and moderation about him is that he is careful to deny one propensity for the sake of indulging another. He hesitates not whether he shall indulge himself, but sometimes hesitates and ponders and deliberates with respect to the particular propensity to be indulged or denied. He is at all times perfectly reckless in regards to self-indulgence. This is settled. Whenever he hesitates about any given course, it is because of the strength of the self-indulgent spirit and with intention, on the whole, to realize the greatest amount of self-indulgence.

When sinners hesitate about remaining in sin and think of giving up self-indulgence, it is only certain forms of sin that they contemplate relinquishing. They consider what they shall lose to themselves by continuing in sin, and what they shall gain by relinquishing their sin and turning to God. It is a question of loss and gain with them. They have no idea of giving up every form of selfishness; nor do they consider that until they do, they are at every moment violating the whole law, whatever interest of self they may be plotting to secure, whether the interest is temporal or eternal, physical or spiritual.

In respect to the denial or indulgence of one or another of

the propensities, such action, by necessity, will be consistent with the nature of selfishness. But in respect to duty, to the commands and threatenings of God, to every moral consideration, they are entirely and universally reckless. And when they appear to not be so, but to be thoughtful and considerate, it is only selfishness plotting its own indulgence and calculating its chances of loss and gain. Indeed it would appear, when we take into consideration the known consequences of every form of selfishness, and the sinner's pertinacious cleaving to self-indulgence in the face of such considerations, that every sinner is appallingly reckless, and that it may be said that his recklessness is infinite.

FOR REFLECTION

I have decided to follow Jesus, and I will not be swayed by every wind of doctrine. I will think things through, and seek to live for the benefit of God and the universe rather than live in moral insanity and reckless abandon.

21

LOVE IS KIND

"Love is patient, love is kind. It does not envy, it does not boast, it is not proud" (1 Cor. 13:4).

Kindness is another attribute of love. The original word rendered kindness is sometimes rendered gentleness. This term means that state of heart that produces a gentleness and kindness of outward demeanor toward those around us. Benevolence is goodwill. It must possess the attribute of kindness or gentleness toward its object. Love seeks to make others happy. Love is convinced that the beloved object should be treated kindly and gently unless circumstances and character demand a different treatment.

A conduct which disregards the feelings of those around us indicates a very decided and detestable selfish state of mind. Love always manifests a tender regard for the feelings and well-being of its object. Since benevolence is universal love, it will and must manifest the attribute of gentleness and kindness toward all, except in those cases when either the good of the individual or of the public shall demand a different treatment. In such cases it will be only love that leads to different treatment; and in no case will benevolence treat any, even the worst of beings, more severely than is demanded by the highest good.

Benevolence is a unit. It does everything for one reason. It has and must treat all beings kindly unless the public good demands a different course. It punishes, but when it does punish, it does so for the same reason that it forgives, when it does forgive. It gives life and takes it away. It gives health and sickness, poverty and riches. It smiles and frowns. It blesses and curses, and does and says and omits, gives and withholds everything for one and the same reason, that is, the promotion of the highest good of being. It will be gentle or severe as occasions arise which demand either of these exhibitions. Kindness is its rule, and severity is its exception. Both, however, as we shall soon see, are equally and necessarily attributes of benevolence.

The gentleness and kindness of God and of Christ are strikingly manifested in providence and grace. Christ is called a Lamb, no doubt, because of the gentleness and kindness of His character. He is called the Good Shepherd and represented as gently leading His flock and carrying the lambs in His bosom. Many such touching representations are made of Him in the Bible, and He often makes the same manifestation not only in His actual treatment of His servants, but also of His enemies. Who has not witnessed this? And who cannot testify to this attribute of His character as being a thousand times affectingly manifested in his own life? Who can call to mind the dealings of his Heavenly Father without being deeply penetrated with the remembrances not only of His kindness, but His *loving-kindness,* and tender mercy, its exceeding greatness? There is a multitude of tender representations in the Bible which are all verified in the experience of every saint. "As the eagle stirreth up her nest, fluttereth over her young, spreadeth abroad her wings, taketh them, beareth them on her wings: so the Lord alone did lead him and there was no strange God with him" (Deut. 32:11–12). This lovely attribute will and must always appear where benevolence is. It is important, however, to note that natural temperament will often greatly modify the expression of it. "Love is kind." This is one of its attributes; yet as I just said, its manifestations will be modified by one's temperament, education, etc. A manifest absence of it in cases where it would be appropriate is sad evidence that benevolence is lacking.

FOR REFLECTION

I will be kind to friends and enemies alike, knowing of God's great kindness to me and all others, even when we were undeserving of it. I will use kindness and be loving especially in those cases when I have to insist that truth and justice prevail for the sake of an individual and society.

22

LOVE IS SEVERE

"As we have already said, so now I say again: If anybody is preaching to you a gospel other than what you accepted, let him be eternally condemned" (Gal. 1:9).

Severity is another attribute of love. "Behold," says the Apostle, "the goodness and severity of God." They greatly err who assume that love and benevolence are gentle under all circumstances. Severity is not cruelty, but is love manifesting strictness, rigor, and purity when occasion demands. Love is universal goodwill, or willing the highest good of being in general. When, therefore, anyone or any number so conduct themselves as to interfere with and endanger the public good, severity is just as natural and as necessary to benevolence as kindness and forbearance under other circumstances. Christ is not only a Lamb, but also a Lion. He is not only gentle as mercy, but stern as justice; not only yielding as the tender bowels of mercy, but as inflexibly stern as infinite purity and justice. He exhibits the one attribute or the other as occasion demands. At one time we hear Him praying for His murderers, "Father, forgive them, for they know not what they do" (Luke 23:34). At another time, we hear Him say through an Apostle, "If any man love not our Lord Jesus Christ, let him be accursed" (1 Cor. 16:22). At another time, we hear Him in the person of the Psalmist praying for vengeance on His enemies: "Reproach hath broken my heart, and I am full of heaviness, and I looked for some to take pity, but there was none, and for comforters but I found none. They gave me gall for my meat, and in my thirst they gave me vinegar to drink. Let their table become a snare before them, and that which should have been for their welfare, let it become a trap. Let their eyes be darkened that they see not, and make their loins continually to shake. Pour out thine indignation upon them, and let thy wrathful anger take hold upon them. Let their habitation be desolate, and let none dwell in their tents. Add iniquity [punishment] to their iniquity and let them not come into thy righteousness. Let them be blotted out of the book of the living and not be written with the righteous" (Ps. 69:20–28). Many similar passages might be quoted from the records of inspiration as the breathings of the Spirit of the God of Love.

Now it is perfectly manifest that goodwill to the universe implies opposition to whatever tends to prevent the highest good. Benevolence is and must be severe in a good sense toward incorrigible sinners like those against whom Christ prays in the Psalm just quoted.

The term *severity* is used sometimes in a good and sometimes in a bad sense. When used in a bad sense, it means an unreasonable state of mind and, of course, a selfish state of mind. In the latter it represents a state which is the opposite of benevolence. But when used in a good sense it means the sternness, firmness, purity and justice of love, acting for the public good in cases where sin exists and where the public interests are at stake. In such circumstances, if severity were not developed as an attribute of benevolence, it would demonstrate that benevolence could not be the whole of virtue, even if it could be virtue at all. The intelligence of every moral being would affirm in such circumstances that if severity did not appear, something was lacking to make the character perfect— that is, to make the character answerable to the emergency.

It is truly amazing to witness the tendency among people to fasten upon a certain attribute of love and overlook the others. Perhaps they have been affected particularly by the manifestation of a certain attribute, which leads them to represent the character of God as all summed up in that attribute. But this is to misrepresent God totally. God is represented in the Bible as being slow to anger, and of tender mercy; as being very pitiful; long-suffering; abundant in goodness and truth; keeping mercy for thousands; forgiving iniquity, transgressions, and sin; but as also visiting the iniquity of the fathers upon the children, and that will by no means clear the guilty; and as being angry with the wicked every day. These are by no means contradictory representations. They only exhibit benevolence manifesting itself under different circumstances, and in different relationships. These are just the attributes we can see that must belong to benevolence, and just what it ought to be and must be when these occasions arise. Goodwill to the universe ought to be and must be, in a good sense, severe where the public welfare demands it, as it often does. It is one of the most prevalent misconceptions that the divine character is all softness and sweetness in all His manifestations and in all circumstances. The fact is that sin has "enkindled a fire in the Divine anger that shall set on fire the foundations of the mountains and shall burn to the lowest hell."

Severity is also always and necessarily an attribute of benevolence in good angels and in good people. When occasions arise that plainly demand it, this attribute must be developed and manifested or benevolence must cease. Indeed, it is impossible that goodwill to the whole should not manifest severity and indignation to a part, those who would rebel against the interests of the whole. Benevolence will seek the good of all so long as there is hope. It will bear and forbear, and be patient, kind, meek even to long-suffering, while there is not a manifestation of incorrigible wickedness. But where there is, the Lamb is laid aside and the Lion is manifested; and His "wrathful anger" is as awful as His tender mercies are moving.

Innumerable instances of this are on record in the world's history. Why then should we seek to represent God's character as consisting of one attribute? Indeed, it is all comprehensively expressed in one word, love. But it should be forever remembered that this is a word of vast importance, and that this love possesses, and as occasions arise, develops and manifests a great variety of attributes—all harmonious, perfect, and glorious.

This attribute of severity always develops itself in the character of holy people when occasions arise that demand it. Remember the severity of Peter in the case of Ananias and Sapphira. Take for example the rebuke administered by Paul to Peter when the latter behaved hypocritically and endangered the purity of the church. Witness also his severity in the case of Elymas, the sorcerer, and hear him say to the Galatians, "I would that they who trouble you were even cut off," and many similar things in the conduct and spirit of holy people.

Now, I know that such actions are sometimes regarded as un-Christlike, as legal, and not evangelical. But they are evangelical. These are only manifestations of an essential attribute of benevolence, as everyone must see who will consider the matter. It very often happens that such manifestations, whatever the occasion may be, are denounced as the manifestations of a wicked spirit, as anger, and as sinful anger. Indeed, it seems to be assumed by many that every kind and degree of anger is sinful. But this is so far from the truth, that occasions often, or at least sometimes, arise that call for such manifestations of anger; and to be any otherwise than indignant, to manifest anything other than indignation and severity, would be to manifest anything but that which is demanded by the occasion.

I know that this truth is liable to abuse in a selfish world. But I also know that it is a truth of revelation; and God has not withheld it for fear of its being abused. It is a truth of reason, and commends itself to the intuitions of every mind. It is a truth abundantly manifested in the moral and providential government of God. Let it not be denied nor concealed; but let no one abuse and pervert it.

FOR REFLECTION

I will boldly stand for what is right and true, and when love demands that I fight against evil, I will fight. However, I will make every effort to fight with a loving and caring attitude for the cause of God in the universe.

23

LOVE IS MODEST

"But mark this: There will be terrible times in the last days. People will be lovers of themselves, lovers of money, boastful, proud, abusive, disobedient to their parents, ungrateful, unholy, without love, unforgiving, slanderous, without self-control, brutal, not lovers of the good, treacherous, rash, conceited, lovers of pleasure rather than lovers of God—having a form of godliness but denying its power. Have nothing to do with them" (2 Tim. 3:1–5).

Modesty is another attribute of love, and it may exist either as a phenomenon of the emotions or of the will.

As a phenomenon of the emotions, it consists in a *feeling* of sensitivity or shrinking from whatever is impure, unchaste; or from all boasting, vanity or egotism; a feeling like retiring from public observation, especially from public applause. It is a feeling of self-diffidence, the opposite of self-esteem and self-complacency. Modesty, as a mere feeling, takes on a great variety of types, and when it controls the will, often gives its subject a very lovely and charming exterior. This is especially true when manifested by a female. But when this is only a phenomenon of the emotions, and manifests itself only as this feeling takes control of the will, it is not virtue but only a misleading and delusive form of selfishness. It appears lovely because it is the counterfeit of a sweet and charming form of virtue.

As a phenomenon of the will and as an attribute of benevolence, it is a disposition which opposes display and self-exaltation. It is closely related to humility. It is a state of heart which is the opposite of an egotistical spirit. Modesty does not seek personal applause or distinction. It is the unostentatious characteristic of benevolence. "Love seeketh not its own, is not puffed up, doth not behave itself unseemly." Benevolence does not seek its own profit, nor its own honor. It seeks the good of being, with a single eye, and has no intention whatsoever to set off self for some advantage. Hence, modesty is one of its lovely characteristics. It manifests itself very much as the feeling of modesty manifests itself when it takes control of the will, so that often it is difficult to distinguish modesty as a virtue, or as an attribute of religion, from that modesty of feeling which is a peculiarity of the temperament of some, and which comes to control the will.

True piety is always modest. It is unassuming, unostentatious, anti-egotistical, content to seek with a single eye its object—the highest good of being. In this work it does not seek public notice or applause. It finds a luxury in doing good no matter how unobserved. If at any time it seeks to be known, it is entirely disinterested in its intention. It seeks to be known only to make "manifest that its deeds are wrought in God," and to stimulate and encourage others to good works. Modesty as a virtue shrinks from self-display, from trumpeting its own deeds. This virtue is prone to "esteem others better than self," to give the preference to others, and hold self in very moderate estimation. It is the opposite of self-confidence and self-exaltation. It aims not to exhibit self, but God and Christ.

This form of virtue is often noticeable in people whom the providence of God has given prominent positions, so that they are exposed to the public gaze. They never seem to aim at the exhibition or exaltation of self; they never appear flattered by applause, nor to be disheartened by censure and abuse. Having this attribute largely developed, they pursue their way very much regardless of both the praise and censure of others. Like Paul they can say, "With me it is a small thing to be judged of man's judgment." It seeks only to commend itself to God and to the *consciences* of people.

Gratitude is another characteristic of love. Sometimes gratitude also means a state of the emotions, or a mere feeling of being obliged or benefited by another. This feeling includes an emotion of love and attachment to the benefactor who has shown us favor. It also includes a feeling of obligation and readiness to make such returns as we are able to the one who has shown us favor. But as a mere feeling, or phenomenon of the sensibility, gratitude has no moral character. It may exist in the emotions of one who is entirely selfish. For selfish people love to be obliged, and love those who love to oblige them, and can *feel* grateful for favors shown to themselves.

Gratitude, as a virtue, is only a modification or an attribute of benevolence or of goodwill. It consists in willing good to a benefactor either of ourselves or of others because of the favor bestowed. Gratitude always assumes, of course, the intrinsic value of the good willed as the fundamental reason for willing it. But it always has particular reference to the relation of benefactor as a secondary reason for willing good *to him*.

This relation cannot be the foundation of the obligation to love or will the good of any being in the universe; for the obligation to will his good would exist even if this relation did not exist, and even if the relation of persecutor existed in its stead. But gratitude, always assuming the existence of the fundamental reason—that is, the intrinsic value of the well-being of its object for its own sake—has particular reference to the relation of benefactor. In fact, if asked why he loved or willed the good of that individual, he would naturally specify this particular relation as a reason. He would, as has been formerly shown, specify this as the reason, not because it is or can be or ought to be the fundamental reason, but because the other reason exists in the mind as a first truth, and is not so much consciously noticed at the time as the secondary reason, that is, the relation just referred to.

This attribute of benevolence may never have occasion for its exercise in the divine mind. No one can sustain to God the relationship of benefactor. Yet in His mind it may and no doubt does exist in the form of goodwill to those who are the benefactors of others, and for that reason, just as finite minds, may be affected by that relationship.

Whether love will ever have an opportunity to develop all its attributes and manifest all its loveliness and take on every possible peculiarity is more than we can know. All its loveliness can never be known nor conceived of by finite minds except so far as occasions present opportunities to develop its charming attributes. The love of gratitude finds abundant occasions of development in all finite minds, especially among sinners. Our just punishment is so infinite, and God's goodness, mercy, and long-suffering are so infinite and so manifested to us, that if we have any attribute of benevolence largely developed, it must be that of gratitude. Gratitude to God will manifest itself to God in a spirit of thanksgiving, and in a very tender regard for His feelings, His wishes, and all His commandments. A grateful soul will naturally raise the question on all occasions, Will this or that please God? There will be a constant endeavor of the grateful soul to please Him. This must be; it is the natural and inevitable result of gratitude. It should always be remembered that gratitude is goodwill modified by the relationship of benefactor. It is not a mere feeling of thankfulness, but will always produce that feeling. It is a living, energizing attribute of benevolence and will and must manifest itself in corresponding feeling and action.

It should also be remembered that a selfish feeling of gratitude or thankfulness often exists, and imposes upon its subject and often upon others who witness its manifestation. It conceals its selfish foundation and character and passes in this world for virtue; but it is not. I recollect well weeping with gratitude to God years previous to my conversion. The same kind of feeling is often, no doubt, mistaken for evangelical gratitude.

Benevolence is a unifying principle. The benevolent soul regards all interests as his own and all beings as parts of himself in such a sense as to feel obligations of gratitude for favors bestowed on others as well as himself. Gratitude, as an attribute of benevolence, recognizes God as a benefactor to self in bestowing favors on others. In regarding all interests as our own, benevolence acknowledges the favors bestowed upon any and upon all. It will thank God for favors bestowed upon the beasts of the field and the fowls of the air, and for "opening his hand and supplying the wants of every living thing."

FOR REFLECTION

I am grateful to God for all that He has done for me. I thank Him for life, and for the gift of life eternal through His Son Jesus Christ. I am grateful to God, my Father, for the gift of His Spirit who lives in me. I will always see who I am in the light of what He has done, so that I will have no reason to boast. And I will ask His Spirit to help me make an honest assessment of myself and where I stand, especially when I receive praise or blame from other people.

24

LOVE IS SOBER

"See that what you have heard from the beginning remains in you. If it does, you also will remain in the Son and in the Father. And this is what he promised us—even eternal life" (1 John 2:24–25).

Sobriety is another attribute of love. Sobriety as a virtue is the opposite of levity. There is, as everyone knows, a remarkable difference in the temperament of different people whose levity and sobriety are a tendency of the emotions. Sobriety as a constitutional peculiarity is often attributable to a physical illness, and is then often termed hypochondriasis. In other instances it seems not to result from or to indicate illness, but is a peculiarity which cannot be explained by any philosophy. Sobriety as an expression of the emotions often results from conviction of sin and fear of punishment, from worldly troubles, or from many other causes.

But sobriety as a virtue and as an attribute of benevolence is solemn earnestness which rises from an honest intention to pursue to the utmost the highest good of being.

Sobriety is not synonymous with *gloominess*. It is not a sour, fault-finding, censorious spirit. Neither is it inconsistent with cheerfulness, i.e., the cheerfulness of love. It is the opposite of levity, and not of cheerfulness. Sobriety is serious earnestness in the choice and pursuit of the highest good of being. It has no heart for levity and folly. It cannot enjoy the spirit of gossip and of giggling. Sober earnestness is one of the essential attributes of love for God and souls. It cannot fail to manifest this characteristic.

Benevolence supremely values its object. It meets with many obstacles in attempting to secure it. It also deeply prizes the good of being, and sees too plainly how much is to be done to have any time or inclination for levity and folly.

God is always in serious earnest. Christ was always serious and in earnest. Trifling is an abomination to God and to benevolence also.

But never forget that sobriety as an attribute of love has nothing in it of the nature of gloominess and peevishness. It is not melancholy, sorrowfulness, nor despondency. It is a sober, honest, earnest, intense state of choice, of goodwill. It is not an affected but a perfectly natural and serious earnestness.

Benevolence is in earnest and it appears to be so by a law of its own nature. It does not affect solemnity. It needs none. It can laugh and weep for the same reason and at the same time. It can do either without levity on the one hand and without gloominess, melancholy or discouragement on the other. Abraham fell on his face and laughed when God promised him a son by Sarah. But it was not levity. It was love rejoicing in the promise of a faithful God.

Always be careful to distinguish between the sobriety of mere feeling and the sobriety of the heart. The former is often easily spent and succeeded by trifling and levity; the latter is stable as benevolence itself because sobriety is one of its essential attributes. A trifling Christian is a contradiction. It is as absurd as a light and foolish benevolence. These are equivalent to a sinful holiness.

Benevolence has and must have its changeless attributes. Some of them are manifest only on particular occasions that reveal them. Others are manifest on all occasions as every occasion calls them into exercise. This attribute, sobriety, is one of that class. Benevolence must be in serious earnest on all occasions. The benevolent soul may and will rejoice with those who rejoice and weep with those who weep. He may always be cheerful in faith and in hope, yet he always has too great business on hand to have a heart for trifling or for folly.

Intemperance, the opposite of sobriety, is a form or attribute of selfishness. Selfishness is self-indulgence, the committal of the will to the indulgence of the desires. One or more of the propensities have taken control of the will. Generally the influence of some ruling passion or desire overshadows and overrules the will for its own gratification. Sometimes it is acquisitiveness or avarice, the love of gain. Sometimes it is love of food or epicurianism. Sometimes it is love of sensual or sexual love. Sometimes it is love of one's own children. Sometimes it is self-esteem or self-confidence. Sometimes it is another of the great variety of tendencies which is so well developed that it becomes a ruling tyrant, lording over the will and over all the other propensities. It matters not whether one of the tendencies or their united influence gains the mastery of the will; whenever the will is subject to them, this is selfishness. It is the carnal mind.

Intemperance is the undue or unlawful indulgence of any tendency or emotion. Therefore, it is an essential element or attribute of selfishness. All selfishness is intemperance. Of course, it is an unlawful indulgence of the propensities. Intemperance has as many forms as there are natural and artificial appetites to gratify. A selfish mind cannot be temperate. If one or more of the tendencies is restrained, it is only restrained for the sake of the undue and unlawful indulgence of another. Sometimes the tendencies are intellectual, and the bodily appetites are denied for the sake of gratifying the love of study. But this is no less intemperance and selfishness than the gratification of sensuality or love of food. Selfishness is always and necessarily intemperate. It does not always or generally develop every form of intemperance in the outward life, but a spirit of self-indulgence must be the spirit of intemperance.

Some develop intemperance most prominently in the form of self-indulgence in eating; others in sleeping; others in lounging and idleness; others in gossiping; others in exercise; others in study (thus impairing health and inducing derangement or seriously impairing the nervous system). Indeed, there is no end to the forms which intemperance assumes because of the great number of tendencies, natural and artificial, that in their turn seek and obtain indulgence.

Always bear in mind that any form of self-indulgence is equally an instance of selfishness and wholly inconsistent with any degree of virtue in the heart. But it may be asked, Are we to have no regard whatever for our tastes, appetites, and tendencies? I answer that we must never allow their gratification to become the goal for which we live, even for a moment. But there is a kind of regard for them which is lawful and therefore a virtue. For example, suppose I am on a journey for the glory of God. Two ways are before me. One affords nothing to pleasure the senses; the other conducts me through multi-hued scenery, sublime mountain passes, deep ravines, along brawling brooks and meandering rivulets, through beds of gayest flowers and woods of richest foliage, through aromatic groves and forests vocal with feathered songsters. The two paths are equal in distance and in all other respects are relevant to the business I have at hand. Now reason dictates and demands that I should take the path that is most enjoyable and edifying.

This is not governed by the inner urges, however, but by the reason. It is the voice of reason which I hear and to which I listen when I take the sunny path. The delights of this path are really good. As such they are not to be despised or neglected. But if taking this path would embarrass and hinder the end or goal of my journey, I am not to sacrifice the greater public good for a lesser one of my own. I must not be guided by my feelings, but by my reason and honest judgment in this and in every case of duty.

God has not given us tendencies or desires to be our masters and to rule us, but to be our servants and to give us enjoyment when we obey the biddings of reason and of God. They are given to make duty pleasant and to reward virtue, to make the ways of wisdom pleasant. The tendencies are not, therefore, to be despised, nor is their annihilation to be desired. Nor is it true that their gratification is always selfish. But when their gratification is sanctioned and demanded, as in the case supposed above and in myriads of other cases that occur to the intelligence, the gratification is not a sin but a virtue. It is not selfishness, but benevolence. But remember that the indulgence must not be sought in obedience to the propensity itself, but in obedience to the law of reason and of God. When reason and the will of God are not consulted, selfishness results.

Intemperance, as a sin, is not the outward act of indulgence, but the inward disposition. A dyspeptic (one suffering from indigestion) who can eat only enough to sustain life may be an enormous glutton at heart. He may have an indulgent disposition; that is, he may not only *desire,* but he may be *willing* to eat all before him—except for the pain indulgence causes him. But this is merely the spirit of self-indulgence. He denies himself the amount of food he craves in order to avoid pain or to gratify a stronger tendency, the dread of pain.

Similarly, a man who was never intoxicated in his life may be guilty of the crime of drunkenness every day. He may be prevented from drinking to inebriation every day only by a regard for reputation or health, or by an avaricious disposition. It is only because he is prevented by the greater power of some other propensity. If a person refuses to indulge certain appetites without restraint only because this would be inconsistent with the indulgence of the others, he is just as guilty as if he were to indulge them all. For example, suppose he has a disposition or a will to accumulate property. He is therefore avaricious in heart. He also has a strong tendency to luxury, immorality and reckless spending. The indulgence of these propensities is inconsistent with the indulgence of avarice. But for this conflict, he would like to indulge them all. Therefore, he is guilty of all those forms of vice, and just as blameworthy as if he indulged in them.

The following list reveals that selfishness is the aggregate of all sin and that he who is selfish is actually chargeable with breaking the whole law, and of every form of iniquity:

1. Selfishness is the committal of the will to self-indulgence, naturally and of necessity.

2. No one propensity will be denied except for the indulgence of another.

3. If no other reason exists for denying any propensity, or tendency, then the selfish person is chargeable in the sight of

God with gratifying in heart every tendency.

4. And this leads to the plain conclusion that a selfish person is full of sin and actually in heart guilty of every possible or conceivable abomination.

5. "Whosoever looketh on a woman to lust after her hath committed adultery with her already in his heart" (Matt. 5:28). He may not have committed the outward act for lack of opportunity, or for the reason that the indulgence is inconsistent with the love of reputation or fear of disgrace, or with some other tendency. Nevertheless, he is in heart guilty of the deed.

Intemperance as a crime is a state of mind. It is the attitude of the will. It is an attribute of selfishness. It consists in the choice or disposition to gratify the tendencies or desires regardless of the law of benevolence. This is intemperance; and so far as the mind is considered, it is the whole of it. Now if the will is committed to self-indulgence, and only the conflict between desires prevents the unlimited indulgence of them all, it follows that every selfish person, or in other words every sinner, is chargeable in the sight of God with every kind of intemperance, actual or conceivable. His lusts have the reign. They conduct him wherever they blow. He has sold himself to self-indulgence. If there is any form of self-indulgence that is not developed in him, he deserves no credit. The providence of God has restrained the outward indulgence, though in him there has been a readiness to do it.

FOR REFLECTION

I will enjoy life and the multitude of blessings God has provided in the world He has created, but this enjoyment will never become a selfish end in itself or the goal of my life.

25

LOVE IS SINCERE

"The Word became flesh and lived for a while among us. We have seen his glory, the glory of the one and only Son, who came from the Father, full of grace and truth" (John 1:14).

Sincerity is another attribute of love. Sincerity is the opposite of hypocrisy. *Sincerity* and *perfection* seem to be synonymous as they are used in the Bible. Sincerity as an attribute of benevolence implies a wholehearted honesty, singleness of aim, uprightness of purpose.

Where this attribute exists, there is a consciousness of its presence. The soul is satisfied that it is truly wholehearted. It cannot but respect its own honesty of purpose. It need not *feign* sincerity—it *has* it. When the soul has developed this attribute, it is as deeply conscious of wholeheartedness as of its own existence. It is honest, earnest, and deeply sincere. It *knows* it, and never thinks of being suspected of insincerity, and of course has no reason for pretense.

This also is an attribute of benevolence which manifests itself on all occasions. The manifestation of sincerity carries conviction in the spirit and conduct of the truly benevolent person. It is so difficult to counterfeit sincerity that the deception can usually be seen. The very attempt to counterfeit sincerity will manifest hypocrisy to a discerning mind. There is an affected tone of voice, a grimace, a put-on seriousness, a hollow, shallow, long-facedness that reveals a lack of sincerity; and the more pain is taken to cover up insincerity, the more surely it reveals itself.

There is a simplicity and unguardedness, a frankness, an openheartedness, a transparency in sincerity that is charming. It tells the whole story, and carries with it on its very face the demonstration of its honesty. Sincerity is its own passport, its own letter of commendation. It is transparent as light and as honest as justice, as kind as mercy and as faithful as truth. It is all lovely and praiseworthy. It needs no hoods or gowns or canonicals or ceremonials to set it off. It stands on its own foundation. It walks abroad unsuspecting, and generally unsuspected, of hypocrisy. It lives and moves and has its being in open daylight. It inhabits love as its dwelling place; and where benevolence is, there is its rest.

FOR REFLECTION

I will manifest transparent honesty and sincerity in my relationships with others, because I will treat all people according to the grace and truth Jesus Christ has shown me.

26

LOVE IS ZEALOUS

"Let us not become weary in doing good, for at the proper time we will reap a harvest if we do not give up. Therefore, as we have opportunity, let us do good to all people, especially to those who belong to the family of believers" (Gal. 6:9–10).

Zeal is another attribute of love. Zeal is not always a phenomenon of the will, because this term often expresses an effervescing state of the emotions. It often expresses enthusiasm in the form of excited feeling. Zeal is also often an attribute of selfishness. The term expresses intensity, whether used of the will or of the emotions, whether designating a characteristic of selfishness or of benevolence.

Benevolence is an intense action of the will or an intense state of choice. The intensity is not uniform, but varies according to perceptions of the intellect. When the intellectual grasp of truth is clear, when the Holy Spirit shines on the soul, the actings of the will become proportionately intense. This must be, or benevolence must cease altogether. Benevolence is the honest choice of the highest good of being as an end. Of course it has no sinister or selfish goals to prevent it from laying just that degree of stress upon the good of being which its importance seems to demand. Benevolence is yielding up the will unreservedly to the demands of the intelligence. Nothing else is benevolence. Hence, it follows that the intensity of benevolence will and must vary with varying light. When the light of

God shines strongly upon the soul, there is often a consuming intensity in the action of the will, and the soul can adopt the language of Christ, "The zeal of thine house hath eaten me up" (John 2:17).

In even the most simple-minded person benevolence is zealous. That is, the intellectual perceptions never sink so low that love becomes a stagnant pool. It is never lazy, never sluggish, never inactive. It is aggressive in its nature. It is essential activity. It consists in choice, the supreme choice of an end—in consecration to that end. Zeal, therefore, must be one of love's essential attributes.

A lazy love is a misnomer. In a world where sin exists, benevolence must be aggressive. In such a world it cannot be conservative. It must be disposed to reform. This is its essential nature. A conservative, anti-reform benevolence is sheer selfishness. To baptize anti-reform and conservatism with the name of Christianity is to steal a robe of light to cover the black shoulders of a fiend. Zeal, the zeal of benevolence, will not, cannot, rest while sin exists in the world. God is represented as clothed with zeal as with a cloak; and after making some of His exceeding great and precious promises, He concludes by saying, "The zeal of the Lord of Hosts will perform this" (Isa. 9:7).

FOR REFLECTION

I will love to the point of aggressively doing what is right in opposition to what is wrong. I will pray for the strength, power, and zeal of the Holy Spirit to guide my thoughts, words and actions as I work to overthrow sin in the world.

27

LOVE IS UNITED

"Likewise every good tree bears good fruit, but a bad tree bears bad fruit. A good tree cannot bear bad fruit, and a bad tree cannot bear good fruit" (Matt. 7:17–18).

Unity describes the character of both love and selfishness. Benevolence or love has but one end, and so does selfishness. Love consists in one choice, one ultimate intention. It is always one and indivisible. It possesses many attributes or characteristics, but they are all many phases of one principle. Every modification of virtue, actual or conceivable, may be and must have its origin in love, for in fact it is only a modification of love.

It is easy to see that an honest choice of the highest good of being *as an end* will fully account for every form in which virtue has appeared, or ever can appear. The love or goodwill of God is a unit. He has but one end. All He does is for one and the same reason. So it must be with love in all beings. God's conduct is all equally good and equally praiseworthy:

1. Because He always has one intention.

2. Because He always has the same degree of light or knowledge of truth.

With people this light varies, and consequently they, although benevolent, are not always equally praiseworthy. Their virtue increases as their light increases, and must forever do so if they continue benevolent. But their intent is always one and the same. In this respect their virtue never varies. They have the same end that God has.

If the unity of virtue should be misunderstood, that which really constitutes its essence is overlooked. If it is assumed that there can be various sorts of virtue, this is a fatal mistake. The fact is, virtue consists in wholehearted consecration to one end, and that end is, as it ought to be and must be, the highest well-being of God and of the universe. This and nothing else is virtue. It is identical in all moral agents, in all worlds, and to all eternity. It can never be changed. It can never consist in anything else. God could not alter its nature, nor one of its essential attributes.

The question and the only question is: For what end do I live? To what end am I consecrated? Not, how do I feel, and what is my outward conduct? These may indicate the state of my will, but cannot settle the question! If a person knows anything, it must be that he knows what his supreme intention is. That is, if he considers at all the grand aim of his mind, he cannot fail to see whether he is really living for God and the universe or for himself.

If God is love, His virtue or love must be a unit. If all the law is fulfilled in one word, love, and if love is the fulfilling of the law, then all virtue must have its origin itself in love. And this unity is and must be an attribute of love.

Just as love is a unit, all sin is a unit. That is, there are not various kinds of sin, or various kinds of selfishness, or, strictly speaking, various forms of selfishness. Selfishness is always but one thing. It has but one end and not diverse ends. The indulgence of one appetite or passion, or another, does not imply different ends or forms of selfishness, strictly speaking. It is only one choice, or the choice of one end; the different forms are only the use of different means to accomplish this one end.

In all honesty, there is but one form of virtue. (When we speak of various forms, we speak loosely and in accommodation to the general notions of mankind.) As we have seen, virtue is a unit. It always consists in ultimate intention; and this ultimate intention is aways one and the same: the choice of the highest well-being of God and of the universe as an end. This intention never changes its form, and all the efforts which the mind makes to realize this end, and which we loosely call different forms of virtue, are really only the one unchanged and unchangeable, uncompounded and indivisible intention, energizing to realize its one great end.

The same is true of selfishness. It is one choice, or the choice of one and only one end: self-gratification or self-indulgence. All the various and ever varying shifts and turns and modes of indulgence which make up the life of the sinner imply no complexity in the form or substance of his choice. He resorts to them all for only one reason. They are only this one uncompounded and uncompoundable, this never varying choice of self-indulgence, energizing and using various means to realize its one simple end.

The reason the idea is so common, and why the phraseology of men implies that there are really various forms of sin and of holiness is that they unwittingly lose sight of the bases of sin and holiness, thinking these belong to the outward act, or to the willful resolve to attain that state. Always remember, however, that holiness and sin are but the moral attributes of benevolence and selfishness, respectively; they are each the choice of one end and only one. Therefore, the delusion that there are various forms and kinds of sin and holiness should flee away forever.

Holiness is in form and essence one and indivisible. It is the moral quality of disinterested benevolence. Sin is in form and essence one and indivisible. It is the moral quality of selfishness, the choice of self-indulgence as the end of life. This leads us to the real meaning of those Scriptures which assert that "all the law is fulfilled in one word, love" (Gal. 5:14, author's paraphrase), that love is the whole of virtue and comprises all that we loosely call the different virtues or different forms of virtue. And it also explains this: "For whosoever shall keep the whole law and yet offend in one point, he is guilty of all" (James 2:10). That is, offending in one point implies commission of all sin. It implies and is selfishness, and this is the whole of sin. Religious teachers must understand this, and no longer think of sin as original and actual; as sins of heart and sins of life; as sins of omission and commission; as sins of licentiousness, gluttony, intemperance, and the like. Such concepts and such phraseology will suffice for those who cannot, or have no opportunity to look deeper into the philosophy of moral government; but it is time that the veil is taken away, and both sin and holiness are laid open to the public gaze.

Do not infer that because there is only one form or kind of sin or of holiness, strictly speaking, that therefore all sin is equally blameworthy, and that all holiness is equally praiseworthy. This does not follow. Neither let it be called a contradiction that I so often speak of the different forms of sin and of holiness. All this is convenient and, as I judge, indispensable in preparing the way, in leading minds to the true understanding of this great and fundamental truth—fundamental in the sense that it lies at the foundation of all truly clear and just conceptions of either holiness or sin. They are both units, and eternal and necessary opposites and antagonists. They can never dwell together or coalesce any more than heaven and hell can be wedded to each other.

FOR REFLECTION

I have chosen to love the Lord my God with all my heart, mind, soul, and strength, and my neighbor as myself. I have consecrated myself to the highest well-being of God and the universe. And to the best of my knowledge, all of my actions promote the goal I have chosen.

28

LOVE IS SIMPLE

"Fear the Lord your God, serve him only and take your oaths in his name. Do not follow other gods, the gods of the peoples around you" (Deut. 6:13–14).

Simplicity is another attribute of love and selfishness. Simplicity means singleness, without mixture, having but one simple end. Because love does not, and cannot, mingle with selfishness, love is simple in its aim. It is and must be simple or single in all its efforts to secure its end. Love does not, cannot, attempt to serve God *and* mammon.

When we speak of simplicity as an attribute of selfishness, we intend two things: It is unmixed and intense. I will consider these two branches of this subject separately and in order.

1. *Selfishness is simple in the sense of being uncompounded or unmixed.*

Selfishness consists, as we have repeatedly seen, in ultimate choice or intention. It is the choice of an end, the supreme, ultimate choice of the soul. Obviously, no other and opposing choice can consist with it. Nor can the mind, while exercising this choice of an end, possibly choose to act inconsistent with it. Willful choices, volitions, can never be made except to secure some end, or in other words, for some reason. If they could, such volitions would have no moral character because there would be no intention. But volitions always imply intention. It is, therefore, impossible that benevolent volitions should coexist with a selfish intention or that selfish volitions should coexist with a benevolent intention.

Simplicity, in the sense of uncompounded or unmixed, must therefore be an attribute of selfishness. This is the philosophy assumed in the teachings of Christ and of inspired Scripture: "No man can serve two masters"—that is, at the same time— "for ye can not serve God and Mammon" (Matt. 6:24), that is, at the same time; and "Doth a fountain send forth at the same place sweet water and bitter?" (James 3:11). Thus we see that the Bible assumes and expressly teaches the philosophy insisted on here.

2. *Selfishness is always as intense as circumstances allow.*

Selfishness is a choice, the choice of self-indulgence as an ultimate goal in life. Therefore, if it lounges, it is only because the tendency to lounge at the time predominates. If it is energetic, it is to secure some form of self-indulgence, which, at the time is preferred to ease. If at one time it is more or less intense than at another, it is only because self-gratification at the time demands it. Indeed, it is absurd to say that it is more intense at one time than at another, except as its intensity is increased by the pressure of motives to abandon it, and become benevolent.

If a selfish person gives himself up to idleness, lounging, and sleeping, it is not for lack of intensity in the action of his will, but because his disposition to self-indulgence in this form is so strong. So if his selfishness takes on any possible type, it is only because of the strength of his disposition to indulge self in that particular way.

Selfishness lives only for one end, and it is impossible for that end, while it continues to be chosen, to not have the supreme control. Indeed, the choice of an ultimate end implies the consecration of the will to it. Therefore, it is a contradiction to say the will is not true to the end which it chooses; it is also a contradiction to say it acts less intensely than is demanded by the nature of the goal and the understanding of the mind concerning the easiest way to realize the goal. The end is chosen without qualification or not at all as an ultimate end. The moment anything should intervene that causes the mind to withhold the energy required to secure it, it would instantly cease to be chosen as an ultimate end. That which has induced the will to withhold the required energy has become the supreme object of regard.

The spirit of self-indulgence will always be as intense as needed to indulge self. The intensity of the spirit of self-indulgence is always at its particular level because, and only because, self is thereby indulged and gratified the most. If the whole self would be more indulged and gratified by greater or less intensity, the intensity must adjust accordingly. The presence of thoughts which would cause benevolence must either annihilate or strengthen selfishness. The selfish choice must be abandoned or its intensity and obstinacy must increase with and in proportion to increasing light. But at every moment the intensity of the selfish choice must be as consistent with the choice of self-indulgence.

FOR REFLECTION

I have repented of selfish and self-indulgent living, and I have turned to serve God with singleness of hope and purpose. I thank Him that He has made this possible through faith in Jesus Christ, and through the power of the indwelling Spirit of Truth.

29

LOVE IS WISE

"However, as it is written: 'No eye has seen, no ear has heard, no mind has conceived what God has prepared for those who love him'—but God has revealed it to us by his Spirit" (1 Cor. 2:9–10).

Wisdom is another attribute of love. Wisdom is love directed by knowledge. It consists in the choice of the best and most valuable end and of the most appropriate means of obtaining it. As all the other attributes, it is only benevolence viewed in a certain relationship or only a particular aspect of it.

"Wisdom" expresses the perfectly intelligent character of love. It represents love as not a blind and unintelligent choice, but as being guided only by the highest intelligence. This attribute, as all the others, is perfect in God in an infinitely higher sense than in any person. It must be perfect in people in such a sense as to be sinless, but can in them never be perfect in such a sense as to admit no improvement.

When duly considered, the many displays of the divine wisdom in creation, providence and grace can overwhelm a finite mind. An inspired apostle celebrated God's wisdom this way: "O the depths of the riches both of the wisdom and knowledge of God! how unsearchable are his judgments, and his ways past finding out!" (Rom. 11:33). The wisdom of the saints appears in their choices of an end. They choose invariably the same end that God does, but do not, for lack of knowledge, always use the best means. This, however, is not a sinful defect in them, provided they act according to the best light within their reach.

Wisdom is a term that is often and justly used to express true religion and to distinguish it from everything else. Wisdom expresses both benevolence or goodwill and the intelligent character of that choice; that is, that the choice is dictated by the intelligence as distinguished from selfish choice or choice occasioned by the impulses of feeling.

FOR REFLECTION

I will make a concerted effort to acquire all the necessary facts before I make a decision, and I will make the best possible decisions and act accordingly within the reasonable limits of time. Motivated by love, I want my decisions and actions to reflect the character of the God I honor as King.

30

LOVE IS GRACIOUS

"What shall we say, then? Shall we go on sinning so that grace may increase? By no means! We died to sin; how can we live in it any longer?" (Rom. 6:1–2).

Grace is another attribute of love. Grace is a disposition to bestow gratuitous favor, i.e., favor on the undeserving and on the ill-deserving. Grace is not synonymous with mercy. It is a term of broader meaning. Mercy is a disposition to forgive the guilty. Grace expresses not only a willingness to pardon, but to bestow other favors. Mercy might pardon, but unless great grace were bestowed our pardon would by no means secure our salvation.

> "Grace first contrived the way
> To save rebellious man;
> And all the steps that grace display
> That drew the wondrous plan."

Grace does not wait for merit as a condition of bestowing favor. Grace causes its sun to shine on the evil and on the good, and sends its rain upon the just and the unjust.

Grace in the saints manifests itself in acts of benevolence to the most unworthy as well as to the deserving. It seeks to do good to all whether they deserve it or not. It seeks to do good from a love to being. It rejoices in opportunities to bestow its free gifts upon all classes that need them. To grace, necessity or lack is the great recommendation.

When we come to God His grace is delighted with the opportunity to supply our wants. The grace of God is a vast ocean without shore or bound or bottom. It is infinite. It is an ever-overflowing ocean of generosity. Its streams flow out to make the universe glad. All people are objects of His grace to a greater or lesser extent. All are not objects of His saving grace, but all are or have been the recipients of His bounty. Every sinner that is kept out of hell is sustained every moment by grace. Everything received that is better than hell, which everyone who has ever sinned deserves, is given by grace.

Repentance is a condition for the exercise of mercy. But grace is exercised in a thousand forms without condition, without any reference to character. Indeed, the very term expresses goodwill to the undeserving and ill-deserving. Surely it must have been a gracious disposition, deep and infinite, that devised and executed the plan of salvation for sinners of our race.

A sympathy with the grace of God must manifest itself in strenuous and self-denying efforts to secure to the greatest possible number of people the benefits of this salvation. A gracious heart in a person will leap forth to declare the infinite riches of the grace of God in the ears of a dying world. Certainly, no one has or can have a sympathy with Christ who will, or can, hesitate to do his utmost to carry the gospel and apply His grace to a perishing world. If the gracious disposition of Christ has prepared the way, prepared the feast, how can someone have any sympathy with Christ if he can hesitate to go or send to invite the starving poor? If Christ both lived and died to redeem sinners, is it a great thing for believers to live to serve sinners? No, indeed. He only has the spirit of Christ who would not merely live, but also die, for them.

FOR REFLECTION

I thank God for His gracious love shown to me in Jesus Christ, and I thank Him that my salvation is made sure through faith in Him. May I be a vessel to pour out His grace and love to all people.

31

LOVE IS ECONOMICAL

"And we know that in all things God works for the good of those who love him, who have been called according to his purpose" (Rom. 8:28).

Economy is another attribute of love. Economy expresses that peculiarity of benevolence that makes the best and the most use of everything to promote the public good. This attribute appears at every step in the works and government of God. It is truly wonderful to see how everything is made and conducted to one end; and nothing exists or can exist in the universe which God will not overrule to some good account. Even "the wrath of man shall praise Him, and the remainder of wrath He will restrain" (Ps. 76:10, author's paraphrase). A divine economy is everywhere manifest in the works and ways of God. If He is love, we might expect this. In fact, if He is love, it is impossible that this should not be so. He lives only for one end. All things were created and are ruled or overruled by Him. All things, then, must directly or indirectly work together for good. He will secure some benefit from everything. Nothing has occurred, or will or can ever occur throughout all eternity, that will not in some way be used to promote the good of being. Even sin and punishment will not be without their use.

God has created nothing in vain, nor has He allowed anything to occur in vain. There is nothing without its use. Sin, inexcusable and ruinous as it is, is not without its use. And God will take care to glorify himself in sinners whether they consent or not, for He has "made all things for himself; yea, even the wicked for the day of evil" (Prov. 16:4). That is, He created no man wicked, but He created those who have become wicked. He created them not for the sake of punishing them, but knowing that they had the potential to become incorrigible sinners, He designed to punish them and, by making them a public example, render them useful to His government. He created them, not because He delighted in their punishment for its own sake, but that He might make their deserved punishment useful to the universe. In this sense, it may be truly said that He created them for the day of evil.

God's glorious economy in cultivating all events for the public good is poignantly displayed in the fact that all things are made to work together for good to those who love God. Saints and sinners, good and evil angels, sin and holiness, and all beings and events in the universe are used up for the promotion of the highest good. Whether people mean good or not, God means it. If people do not mean it, they merit no credit for whatever use God may make of them. He will give them, as He says, according to their endeavors or intentions, but He will take care to use them in one way or another for His glory.

If sinners will consent to live and die for His glory and the good of being, well; they shall have their reward. But if they will not consent, He will dispose of them for the public benefit. He will make the best use of them He can. If they are willing and obedient, if they sympathize with Him in promoting the good of the universe, well. But if not, He can make them a public example, and make the influence of their punishment useful to His kingdom.

Nothing shall be lost; God will make it answer some useful purpose. No, not even sin with all its deformities and guilt, and blasphemy with all its guilt and desolating tendencies shall be allowed to exist in vain. It will be made useful in innumerable ways. But no thanks to the sinner; he means none of his sin to be useful. He is set upon his own gratification regardless of the consequences. Nothing is further from his heart than to do good and glorify God. But God has His eye upon him and has laid

His plans in view of his potential for wickedness; therefore, as surely as Jehovah lives, the sinner in one way or another will be used for the glory of God and the highest good of being.

Economy is, in all minds, necessarily an attribute of love. The very nature of love shows that it must be so. It is consecration to the highest good of being. It lives for no other end. Every choice must respect means or ends. Benevolence has but one end; and all its activity, every choice that it makes, must be to secure that end. The intellect will be used to devise means to promote that end. The whole life and activity of a benevolent being is and must be a life of strenuous economy for the promotion of the one great end of love. Extravagance, self-indulgence, waste, are necessarily foreign to love. Everything is devoted to one end. Everything is scrupulously and wisely directed to secure the highest good of God and being, in general. This is, this must be, the universal and undeviating aim of every mind just so far as it is truly benevolent. "He that hath an ear to hear, let him hear."

FOR REFLECTION

I thank God that He never wavers from pursuing the highest good. I am awed that He uses even my sins and mistakes to reach that end. I thank Him that He will take every sin that I have ever committed and turn it to His glory, and I pray that He will use every talent I have for His benefit.

32

LOVE IS HOLY

"If you love those who love you, what reward will you get? Are not even the tax collectors doing that? And if you greet only your brothers, what are you doing more than others? Do not even pagans do that? Be perfect, therefore, as your heavenly Father is perfect" (Matt. 5:46–48).

Holiness, or *purity,* is another attribute of love. Holiness is a term sometimes used to depict all the moral attributes of God. As an attribute of love, it signifies purity. It denotes the moral purity or moral character or quality of God's benevolence. It also indicates or expresses the intention to promote the happiness of moral beings through moral purity or virtue. Benevolence, or love, is simply a willing or choosing the highest good of being, especially that of moral agents.

Holiness as an attribute of benevolence is that element of the choice that aims to secure the end of benevolence by means of virtue. Moral purity is uprightness or righteousness. Uprightness or integrity are generally synonymous with holiness. Holiness as an attribute of God is commonly assumed and is frequently asserted in the Bible.

As an attribute of God, holiness must be an attribute of love; for God is love. This attribute is celebrated in heaven as one of those aspects of the divine character that give ineffable delight. Isaiah saw the seraphim standing around the throne of Jehovah, crying to one another, "Holy! holy! holy!" (6:3). John also had a vision of the worship of heaven, and says "they rest not day and night saying, Holy, holy, holy, Lord God Almighty" (Rev. 4:8). When Isaiah beheld the holiness of Jehovah he cried out, "Woe is me! for I am undone; because I am a man of unclean lips, and I dwell in the midst of a people of unclean lips: for mine eyes have seen the King, the Lord of hosts!" (Isa. 6:5). God's holiness is infinite; it is, therefore, no wonder that the sight of it should thus affect the prophet.

Finite holiness must forever stand and feel itself to be comparative rottenness and impurity when compared with infinite holiness. The seraphim are shown as being affected as much as the prophet was. At least, had the vision of God's holiness been as new to them as it was to him, it might no doubt have impressed them as it did him. Their holiness in the comparison or light of His might have seemed to them as pollution. They veiled their faces in His presence. They covered their faces as if afraid, or as if they had considered that in His eyes the most holy creatures in the universe were comparatively unclean.

Every Christian of much experience knows well what it is to be confounded in the presence of His awful holiness. Job says, "I have heard of thee by the hearing of the ear: but now mine eye seeth thee. Wherefore I abhor myself and repent in dust and ashes" (Job 42:5, 6). There is no comparing finite with infinite. The time will never come when creatures can behold the awesome holiness of Jehovah without shrinking into comparative rottenness in His presence.

This must be, and yet in another sense they may be and are as holy as He is. They may be as perfectly conformed to what light or truth they have as He is. This is doubtless what Christ intended when He said, "Be ye therefore perfect, even as your Father which is in heaven is perfect" (Matt. 5:48). He meant that they should live to the same end and be as entirely consecrated to it as He is. This they must be to be truly virtuous or holy in any degree. But when they are so, a full view of the holiness of God would still confound and overwhelm them. If anyone doubts this, he has not considered the matter in a proper light. He has not lifted up his thoughts as needed for the contemplation of Infinite Holiness.

No *person*, however benevolent he is, can witness the divine benevolence without being overwhelmed with a clear vision of it. This is no doubt true of every attribute of the divine love. However perfect creature virtue may be, it is finite, and if brought into the light of the attributes of infinite virtue, it will appear as comparative rottenness. Should the most just person on earth or in heaven witness and have a clear understanding of the infinite justice of God, it would no doubt fill him with unutterable awe of Him. Should the most merciful saint on earth or in heaven have a clear perception of the divine mercy in its fullness, it would swallow up all thought and imagination and no doubt overwhelm him. And so also would every attribute of God.

Oh! When we speak of the attributes of God, we often do not know what we say. Should God unveil himself to us, our bodies would instantly perish. "No man," says He, "can see my face and live" (Ex. 33:20, author's paraphrase). When Moses prayed, "Show me thy glory" (Ex. 33:18), God condescendingly hid him in the cleft of a rock, covered him with His hand and passed by, letting Moses see only His back parts. He warned Moses that he could not behold His face, His unveiled glories, and live.

Holiness is an essential attribute of impartial love. The laws of our being and the very nature of benevolence require this. In man holiness manifests itself in great purity of conversation and conduct, in a great loathing of all impurity of flesh and spirit. Let no one profess piety who does not have this attribute developed. The love required by the law of God is pure love. It seeks to make its object happy only by making him holy. It manifests the greatest abhorrence of sin and all uncleanness. In creatures it pants and will always pant and struggle toward infinite purity or holiness. It will never find a resting place where it desires to ascend no higher. As it perceives more and more of the fullness and infinity of God's holiness, it will no doubt pant and struggle to ascend the eternal heights where God sits in light too dazzling for the strong vision of the highest cherubim.

Holiness of heart produces a desire and love of purity in the emotions. The feelings become very alive to the beauty of holiness and to the hatefulness and deformity of all spiritual and even physical impurity. The emotions become ravished with the great loveliness of holiness and unutterably disgusted with the opposite. The least impurity of conversation or of action severely shocks one who is holy. Impure thoughts, if suggested to the mind of a holy being, are highly detestable, and the soul heaves and struggles to cast them out as the most loathsome abominations.

Related to holiness, *virtuousness* or rightness, as I have said, is also an essential attribute of love. Moral rightness is moral perfection, righteousness, or uprightness. Virtuousness must be a moral element or attribute. The term marks its relationship to moral law and expresses its conformity to it.

In the exercise of this love or choice, the mind is conscious of uprightness, or of being conformed to moral law or moral obligation. In other words, it is conscious of being virtuous or holy, of being like God, of loving what ought to be loved, and of consecration to the right end.

Because this choice agrees with the demands of the intelligence, therefore the mind in its exercise is conscious of the approval of that power of the intelligence which we call conscience. The conscience must approve this love, choice, or intention.

Again, because the conscience approves of this choice, therefore there is and must be a corresponding state of the emotions. There is and must be a feeling of happiness or satisfaction, a feeling of contentment or delight in the love that is in the heart or will. This love, then, always produces self-approval in the conscience, and a sense of satisfaction in the emotions. These feelings are often so strong and joyous, that the soul in the exercise of this love of the heart is sometimes moved to rejoice with joy unspeakable and full of glory.

This state of mind does not always and necessarily amount to joy. Much depends on the clarity of the intellectual views, upon the state of the emotions, and upon the manifestations of divine favor to the soul. But when peace or approval of conscience, and consequently a peaceful state of the emotions do not exist, this love is not present. They are connected with it by a law of necessity, and must of course appear on the field of consciousness where it exists. These, then, are implied in obedience to the law of God. Conscious peace of mind and conscious joy in God must exist where true love to God exists.

There are many other attributes of benevolence that might be enumerated and enlarged upon, all of which are implied in entire obedience to the law of God. I hope enough has been said, however, to fix your attention strongly upon the fact that every variation of virtue, actual, conceivable or possible, is only an attribute or form of benevolence. That attribute is always a phenomenon of will and an attribute of benevolence. And where benevolence is, there all virtue is and must be. And if benevolence really exists, every form in which virtue does or can exist must develop itself as its occasions shall arise.

FOR REFLECTION

I will love others by telling them of the need to turn from selfishness to love, and that with the help of Jesus Christ as their Lord and Savior they can walk a life consistent with His will.[1]

---

[1]Those who struggle with living wholly in the will of God will find excellent help in *Principles of Union with Christ*, by Charles G. Finney (Bethany House Publishers, 1985) a devotional guide to knowing Jesus better through His names in the Bible.

33

GOD'S LOVE TO SINNERS
AS SEEN IN THE GOSPEL

"For God so loved the world that he gave his one and only son, that whoever believes in him shall not perish but have eternal life" (John 3:16).

The subject of this great love is God. *God* so loved this world. Hence, God is not a mere intellect, but He is a being capable of loving.

This declaration about God's love is not a mere figure of speech accommodated to our understanding, and hence perhaps meaning less than it seems to mean. No, it is a statement of fact—a fact substantiated by what God has actually *done*. God loved so much that He gave up His only Son—for sinners. Therefore, we know that God *truly loves,* and much more intensely than any person, as He is greater than any.

Who is the object of God's great love?

The great God loves somebody! Who is it? Who is the favored object of His love?

Sinners are apt to think that God is an infinite abstraction, infinitely above themselves, and quite indifferent as to their welfare. But this text declares that God has most surely and most intensely loved this world. This world the Bible says, meaning not this globe, not this round ball of solid matter, but its people—the living, intelligent, moral, yet sinning race that live and have their being here.

But we must look at the nature of this love. What sort of love is it?

We know that sinners hate God, and yet here we are told that God loves them. We must therefore ask, "With what kind of love?" For on this point it is essential to make the proper distinctions, lest we are led to assume God's love to sinners is mere good nature—a soft, spontaneous feeling which has no regard for character. We must understand that God's love toward sinners is no such thing as this.

God's love to sinners is not a love of respect or complacency, for this form of love fastens upon the character. This love is simply delight in the moral character of the other, and it is obvious that God can have no delight in the character of sinners! Their characters are altogether loathsome to Him. Hence, God's love for sinners cannot be a love of their moral character. He can only love them as cognizant or reasoning beings capable of happiness and misery. In other words, His love for them is a sincere regard and an earnest desire for their well-being.

This is similar to parental love. Parents sometimes have very bad children, and yet they love them, bad though they are. They love them in the sense of desiring their welfare and delighting to do them good. The prodigal son was greatly loved in this manner, although he was by no means lovely in his moral character. Many a son of such character has been the object of yearning affection on the part of his parents. They have cheerfully suffered anything that human nature could bear in order to promote the real welfare of their wayward son.

Of this love we have a most striking illustration in the case of David and Absalom. Absalom had artfully and maliciously seized his father's throne, dishonored his father's bed, and sought his father's life. Yet, when David marshalled his little band of faithful men to take the field against this base usurper, his heart yearned over the base monster his son had become and he begged his generals saying, "Deal gently for my sake with the young man, even with Absalom" (2 Sam. 18:5). And when the cruel son was brought back a corpse, David's grief was inconsolable. He refused to be comforted.

So strong were his expressions of sorrow that Joab feared

its influence upon his army, and solemnly rebuked his king for giving indulgence to such feelings in such an emergency: "Thou hast shamed this day the faces of all thy servants, which this day have saved thy life.... For thou hast declared this day, that thou regardest neither princes nor servants: for this day I perceive, that if Absalom had lived, and all we had died this day, then it had pleased thee well" (2 Sam. 18:5–6).

To this rebuke David may have answered, "I have only given vent to the outburstings of a father's heart." And indeed it was only the deep yearnings of a pious father's heart that sought expression in such words and groans: "O my son Absalom, my son, my son Absalom! would to God I had died for thee, O Absalom, my son, my son!" (2 Sam. 18:33). An ungodly son dies in his sins, and a pious father bemoans his awful death in such language as this! We rarely find anything in history that so forcibly illustrates God's love for sinners as does this lamentation of David over Absalom. Under the influence of his strong affection, David seemed almost to overlook the public danger, for when his army went out to battle and the outcome was still uncertain, he bade his officers deal gently for his sake with the young man Absalom.

Now God does not and cannot overlook the public danger through His great love for sinners, and yet He ventures to pardon and forgive under circumstances which may look as if He did. Oh, how truly God's love for sinners is like the love of a father toward a wayward son!

Many suppose that such language as this in our text has no meaning. Oh, how little they understand the facts of the case! It has a meaning deep and sincere, and is no figure of speech by any means. In language so like that of David, the most high God cries out, "How shall I give thee up, Ephraim! how shall I deliver thee, Israel! ... mine heart is turned within me, my repentings are kindled together" (Hosea 11:8). We cannot but see the honest heart-yearnings of one who loves the human race and who is moved to the very depths of His great heart by the pressure of a stern necessity to inflict punishment. See the heart-yearnings of a father evident in the tears and compassionate tones of the king! He would not allow one hair to fall from the head of his guilty son if he could wisely, safely spare him.

He longs to save your forfeited life. And when in the very act of rebellion you fall and He is obliged to drive the chariot-wheels of his government over your prostrate body, he mournfully laments your fall!

Again, this love reaches every individual member of the human race. The declaration can mean nothing less than God loves every human being—without any exception. What a thought is this! And how difficult for sinners to persuade themselves of its truth, especially of its absolute truth in reference to themselves.

Did you ever try to realize this? Did you ever ask yourself, "Is it indeed true that the great God has a deep personal regard for my happiness, like that which an earthly father has toward his son? Can I believe that His love for me is so great that He finds His happiness even in heaven in unwearied concern to secure my personal salvation?" Such is the fact.

The great difficulty with sinners is that their unbelief to-ward God is so great that this conception does not get into their minds at all. Yet it is a truth that sinners greatly need to understand and take home to their hearts.

Again, this love of God for sinners is a patient love—patient even to the extent of long-suffering, long-enduring the most grievous provocations. If any of you, now living in your sins, had any just sense of your sin against God and of your great provocations of His wrath, you would cry out, "How can it be possible for God to have any tender regard for me? How can He not think of me only as an enemy of His to be crushed before Him as a guilty rebel?"

You speak sometimes of the forbearance of parents toward wayward, vicious children, but how far does this fall short of God's forbearance toward sinners! Suppose you are a wicked child toward your parents, so wicked that you have never obeyed them in a single instance. You have always done as badly as you could, and have invariably pursued a course of persecution, opposition, and utter hostility. If such had been your course and character, would you expect forbearance from human parents? Oh no, none but God can be expected to have forbearance equal to such an emergency.

I beg you to look at this case fairly. Suppose a young lady were to enter this school [Oberlin College], and she had always been a trial and a torment to her parents, had never been known to obey them or to do anything to please them. What would you say of her? What would you think of her? If you learned that in spite of everything, her parents had still loved and sought only her best good, would you not admire their spirit as something more than human? But such a daughter who has so abused her parents you would feel was not fit to live. Your spontaneous indignation would cry aloud, "Let her be spewed out from all human society! There is no fit place for such a wretch beneath the light of the sun!"

Now, sinners, I entreat you to apply this honestly to yourselves. You have done nothing but oppose God. You have not yet done the first thing, however small, from a sincere desire to please God! You know that is the truth! And yet God holds you up in existence, holds you from dropping into hell! He represents himself as holding your feet from sliding, as they stand on the slippery places of the sinner's pathway. Ah, how long He has done this very thing! You have regularly abused all the manifestations of His love, and trampled under foot all His commandments. God says, "These things hast thou done, and I kept silence" (Ps. 50:21). But though silent, He has not forgotten. Yet love will wait in its long-suffering patience till it can wait no longer.

Mark also the lowliness of God's love. See how low God's love stoops. Of the great personification of God's love, Jesus Christ, it was said that He "made himself of no reputation, and took upon him the form of a servant" (Phil. 2:7). Jesus was meek and lowly of heart. Such was the condescension of the Son of God! Scarcely if at all less was the condescension of the Infinite Father. Think at how great an expense He provided the means of your salvation. Think of the self-denial to which He submitted. Do you ask, "What did He do?" He gave up to death His only Son. *Gave* Him, freely, not for money but for love.

When Abraham went to offer up Isaac, and had freely shown his purpose of heart to obey God—and trust Him if need be to raise up his slaughtered son from the dead—God said to him,

"By myself have I sworn . . . for thou hast done this thing, and hast not withheld thy son, thine only son: . . . that I will bless thee, and . . . I will multiply thy seed as the stars of the heaven" (Gen. 22:16, 17). It was a strong point in Abraham's case that he did not withhold his only son. So also God did not spare His only Son, but freely gave Him up for an offering. When Abraham brought his only son to the altar and drew the knife, God's angel caught his arm and pointed out a ram as a substitute for the real offering. But when God gave up His only Son, the demands of justice against the sinner took their course upon His substitute, and the innocent victim was brought to the slaughter. Nailed to the cross, He bled, agonized, languished, and died! Was ever love like this?

This aspect of the divine mind is not easily understood by minds as selfish as ours. Even the best of men are hardly an exception to this. How often do we hear them pray that God would bless all their *friends?* Now in some respects it is quite proper that we should pray for our friends, but we should pray no less for our enemies. Christ prayed for His friends, but also for His enemies. If we were in the practice of praying with all our heart for our worst enemies, we could better understand how Christ could die for His enemies.

You may say, "Oh, if I were truly converted, God would love me." True, He would then love you with the love of *friendship.* Now He loves you with the love of compassion. Yet even this you scarcely realize at all. You find it hard to conceive how God should put His Son into the hands of wicked men and let them murder Him that the murderers might be saved! Surely He would convince you, if He could, that in His deepest affection He loves you! He would make this impression so strong on your heart that even when you come to see your sin's greatness you will hold on to the strange truth that God so loves your soul that He gave up the life of His Son for your salvation.

Yet again, God's great love for sinners is a spontaneous love. It was self-moved. None of the lost human race asked for it. God did not find the world on its bended knees imploring Him, but on the contrary found them all in rebellion strong and stern, fiercely struggling to escape God's authority. Yet even so, His love gushed forth toward them in infinite compassion.

God's love is also a persevering love. God's love was not a love which after a few abortive efforts fell back and gave up the struggle to save. It was not like the love of some Christians for the impenitent, who after a few prayers and efforts give up the endeavor, especially when they meet opposition. God's love for the lost in sin is a persevering love, not easily exhausted, a love that many waters cannot quench nor floods drown. Oh, how well for the sinner that it is all this!

God's love is also a holy love. If it were otherwise, it might have sought to save by means that would have jeopardized the interests of His government. It was a critical and difficult undertaking—this effort to rescue the sinner over whom the violated law was poising its thunderbolts. By some means, the demands of the law must be satisfied, and yet the sinner be spared; but it must be in such a way that will make an impression of the awful guilt of sin—of its great wickedness and especially of the purity and holiness of the great Magistrate of the universe.

It will by no means answer the problem to do anything that shall misrepresent His character. On this point there will be the greatest danger when He comes to set aside the execution of the law, throw the doors of mercy wide open, and invite every sinner to come in. But all this danger has been guarded against most fully in the sacrifice of His glorious Son. It was a love blended with holiness and purity that took these precautions, seeing the need of making some demonstrations, which all beings in heaven, earth, and hell should see. God must write it out in such characters as all can read—engrave it as it were on the everlasting rocks so that through all coming ages every mind in the universe may have the entire demonstration in view, showing how much God hated sin, and how sacred He holds His holy law. He made this impression when He gave up His Son to die in the sinner's stead.

At the cross He demonstrated the purity of His love for the sinner. He showed that mere good nature would not save sinners anyhow. He also showed that He cared for the consequences to the stability of His kingdom; there He made the truth stand out in bold relief that He loved His kingdom no less because He loved the lost sinner. The welfare of the holy, of the yet unfallen, must not be jeopardized to save the guilty.

God's love for sinners is also a wakeful, solicitous love. It pities its objects, and sets the heart intently on blessing those it loves. You may have seen Christians in revivals after their hearts had been brought into deep sympathy with Christ for souls. You observed how wakeful, how anxious, how burdened their hearts were. Perhaps they could scarcely eat or sleep through their great concern for the salvation of souls. What made Jesus Christ spend whole nights in prayer? He was sent to redeem a lost world, and the burden of souls lay heavily upon His heart. It was but plain language without a figure of speech when His disciples applied to Him the passage, "The zeal of my house hath eaten me up." A zeal for God had thrown upon His heart such a burden of care and concern which wasted His mortal frame away. The prophet foresaw this when in a vision he said of Him, "His visage was so marred more than any man, and his form more than the sons of men" (Isa. 52:14).

Old age sat on His faded brow before He had scarcely reached thirty. He was an old man in His very youth, for the "zeal of God's house had eaten him up." Oh, the depth of His compassion for the lost whom He came to save! Hear what He says: "I have a baptism to be baptized with, and how am I straitened till it be accomplished!" Oh, that baptism of suffering which for months and years hung heavily upon His heart in the concern of anticipation—and yet love falters not.

Do you understand this? Do you know from any similar experience of your own what this state of mind is? The fact is, those who have never entered into sympathy with this deep benevolent concern for poor lost souls cannot understand the love of God for sinners. To all but those who have had some experience it is a dark and unknown state of mind. But when you sympathize with God in this thing, when you pour out your life and soul for sinners, then you begin to have some just conceptions of what the state is and then you can begin to understand the nature of God's great love for sinners.

God's love, moreover, is full of *pity*. Under its deep emotions,

God is represented as being greatly moved. Hear Him break out in the depth of His feelings, "Is Ephraim my dear son? Is he a pleasant child? For since I spake against him, I do earnestly remember him still; therefore my bowels are troubled for him: I will surely have mercy upon him, saith the Lord" (Jer. 31:20). God is saying, "My feeling was stirred up by Ephraim's provoking sins and I spake against him that I would soon cut him down." But presently parental affection rises up, and a father's heart earnestly remembers him still. Such is the pity of God for sinners. If God had not such pity as this, how could we account for His conduct in sparing sinners so long? How could we comprehend His not long ago hurling every sinner down to hell?

But let's consider the *goal* or *end* sought in this scheme of love. God gave His Son to achieve the end that "whosoever would believe on him should not perish, but should have everlasting life" (John 3:16).

It seems strange to me that Mr. Storrs and those who agree with him should seize upon such expressions as this, and make them teach the annihilation of the wicked. They hold, as perhaps you know, that "perishing" means "annihilation"; hence, the end to be secured by Christ's death is only to save sinners from annihilation and give them an immortal existence. I find in conversation with them that they are led to this belief by their notions of literal interpretation. They hold that all the language of the Bible must be construed literally, and that the literal sense of the word "perish" is annihilation. But in both these views they are entirely mistaken. Not to dwell at present upon the former, let us consider for a moment the latter. The literal sense of the word "perish" is not "annihilation." When matter is said to perish, it only changes its form and mode of existence; it is not annihilated. Indeed, matter so far as we can see knows nothing of annihilation. So Mr. Storrs utterly fails in applying his doctrine of literal sense, even if the doctrine itself were true. Besides, perishing in this text is put in contrast with everlasting life. But this everlasting life is not a mere existence, prolonged forever, by no means; it is eternal, everlasting blessedness. Hence, its opposite must be everlasting misery.

Moreover, if annihilating the wicked would have answered all the purposes of penalty for the transgression of law, and all things considered, God had seen it wise to punish sinners in this way, He could have done it in a moment, and could have created another world of holy beings by only saying, "LET IT BE!" All would have been easy and done immediately. But we cannot see why it should be needful for Christ to die on the cross solely for the purpose of saving sinners from the doom of annihilation.

Hence, we see that the object of Christ's death for sinners is to bring them back into fellowship and harmony with God and holiness—to make them obedient sons again in His great family.

The means of effecting this change in the moral attitude of sinners toward their great and good Father are especially the full revelations which God makes of himself before the very eyes of men through the incarnation of Jesus Christ. Christ came in mortal flesh to live, to labor, to speak and act among men as a man that He might reveal the true character of God to our race. Hence, Christ is called the *Word* of God, because He reveals God to us, as words reveal thought from mind to mind. This is not the only object of Christ's incarnation, but it is one object and a great one.

Let it be understood then that Christ came in human flesh to reveal before our eyes the great love of God, and to make us understand, indeed, all the great moral attributes of God. He gave His only Son to come among us and live among us as a neighbor. Some of you are craftsmen; Christ wrought among His neighbors as a craftsman to teach men what a craftsman should be. He wrought as a son during His adolescence to teach what a dutiful son should be. Then He appeared in public life showing what men should be in this relation. In all these respects He sought to unfold His true character so that as a model, and more particularly as an exemplification of the true God, He might make His abode among men of the utmost possible service.

One of the great objects of the incarnation was to reveal God so that men should renew their confidence in Him. Sin brought with itself doubt and unbelief respecting God, and this doubt and unbelief must be counteracted before the sinner can be saved. People whose hearts indulge enmity always try to vindicate and justify their enmity by believing evil of the hated party. Enmity, no matter how causeless and wrong, leads to suspicion and slander. The mind, troubled with the consciousness of wrong-doing, seeks relief by self-justification, and to gain this relief is compelled to think and believe evil of those it has unjustly wronged. In precisely this relation does the whole human race stand toward God. They are enemies for no reason whatever, and are thus thrown upon the necessity of some means for impeaching the King they causelessly hate. Such sinners, therefore, are in need of revelations from God that will melt their hard hearts under the manifestations of divine love.

As another great means of accomplishing the end in view, Christ must atone for sin so that sin can be freely forgiven. This He did most effectually. In Christ both parties in this great controversy are represented. Human nature was there and also the Divine. God in human flesh met all the demands of the case and satisfied every demand of the emergency.

On our part, *faith* is the grand condition for being saved. The longer I live, the more clearly I see that faith refers especially to the divinity of Christ, embracing practically His *power* to save and fully admitting that the case is one for which no power short of divine is adequate. "Believest thou that I am able to do this?" "Do you believe that I can raise your dead, heal your sick, cast out your demons, remit your sins? Do you believe all this? Then if so, cast yourself on My power to save." The substance of faith then is this: *believing in Christ as the true God and confiding in Him as such.* Faith confides in Him as to all He professes to be and to do. It is presupposed that the mind apprehends the nature and design of God's love, and then faith receives this as truth, believing that Jesus Christ indeed loved *me,* gave himself *for me, died for me* that I might not die but live. Thus each believing soul for itself meets God in Jesus Christ and yields itself up to God in reliance upon His promises. A full unreserved submission seems none too much. With all the heart, the man commits himself to Christ to be used and governed—to be sanctified and to be saved.

Many people treat Christ as if He were a hypocrite. I do not mean they often say so, but in their hearts they think so, and what they think determines their treatment of Him. They really feel as if they could put no confidence in His profession of friendship.

Let me test you concerning this very point. Have you ever realized that Christ came to save you, as truly as if you were the only sinner in the universe? Have you met Him in this relationship, as if you understood that He actually came to save you, yourself alone? This is the true idea of faith. It believes Christ's word of promise and of offered mercy as applying to your own individual soul.

Faith implies a full renunciation of selfishness. Such renunciation is fully involved in the idea of self-committal to God.

Another element of faith should command our particular regard. It not only believes the history of the past respecting Christ, but also embraces especially all that it finds revealed of His present and future relations. Sinners often believe the past without believing unto salvation, for they do not believe the present and the future. They say, "No doubt Christ once lived and ultimately died, but all this took place a great many years ago and a great way off. After His resurrection, He went to heaven," and there the scope of their faith comes to an end. There is nothing fresh and new in it, nothing that touches the great interests of the soul in its own salvation. It is taken up and thought of as any other fragment of ancient history.

But real faith comes nearer home—much nearer. Real faith takes hold of a present Christ, a Savior living now, yes, ever living at God's right hand and ever making intercession there. Did you ever realize that you have been kept out of hell thus long by Christ's intercession? He himself has illustrated the case in the parable of the barren fig tree. "Spare the sinner!" he cries. "Don't cut him down yet. Save him. Let me bring him once more into the house of God and under the sound of the gospel. It may be he will repent. If not, if every hopeful effort fails, then let him be cut down, but not before." Then let none of you sinners suppose that Christ has lost His interest in you:

far from it; He still prays for you, and still holds you up from sinking into hell. You lay down on your bed last night and slept sweetly. Yet, the only reason you did not sink down quickly into hell was not that *you* prayed but that *Christ* prayed. Jesus Christ, when your heart was all prayerless, lifted up His voice in your behalf and cried, "Oh, spare him yet once more—I will carry him up to the house of God again. If this fails, then cut him down!"

If I may reiterate once more, true faith not only expects forgiveness for all the past, but grace for all the future. Its trustful voice says, "His grace shall be sufficient for me as He has said."

REMARKS

1. Faith is a natural condition for your salvation. By this I mean that it is an indispensable condition in the very nature of the case. If you will not credit what Christ says of himself and of the offers of salvation, all else that you may do is of no avail. So says our text. God gave up His Son, not to save all men unconditionally—not to save the externally moral, or the socially amiable, as such; but to save just those who *should believe in Him*. Of course this settles the question and shows conclusively who will and who will not be saved by Jesus Christ.

2. Your selfishness is that which makes it so difficult for you to rightly conceive these things. You never loved your enemies: you never make any sacrifices of your own ease or pleasure for their good—but God does. Hence you find it difficult, if not impossible, to understand God's benevolence. It is so unlike your own selfishness.

Christ prays for you—has done and still does—and yet you are cruelly slow to believe it. But consider how He beheld Jerusalem and wept over it. He had been among them and knew their malignity toward himself. He saw the whole city becoming deeply excited, sharpening their weapons to slay Him; yet now as He was coming in for the last time, close to the final catastrophe, His heart was deeply moved with pity and compassion. He well knew how much they hated Him and yet He cried out, "O Jerusalem, Jerusalem; thou that killest the prophets and stonest them that are sent unto thee, how often would I have gathered thee as a hen does her brood under her wings—but ye would not" (Luke 13:34). Another evangelist says, "He beheld the city and wept over it." He seemed to forget their awful wickedness as if it had never been.

But how can you realize such a state of mind as His? Your selfishness is so great and so controlling that you never have any such feelings yourself toward your enemies. And when you are called on to relinquish your enmity and selfishness, you plead that you can't do it. Hence you are sadly crippled with respect to meeting the condition of faith intelligently. Just as it is one of the most difficult things in the world to make a great liar believe your word however trustworthy, or just as you cannot persuade a great scoundrel or knave into the course of duty. They don't understand the proper force of the motives you present, and more than that, they don't want to admit sound moral truth to their hearts and consciences. A thief always suspects others of theft. On the same principle, it becomes very difficult for a wicked man to have confidence in God's sincerity and goodness. He may admit it in theory, but still he won't believe it and bring it home to his own heart as a reality.

Now look at the case. See what God has done to provide for your salvation, and also see how much He has said and done to lead you to *believe* it—but alas, your heart is still heavy as lead with unbelief! What more can God do to make you realize it? Oh, tell me, what more? Sinners will stand and look on the cross itself, and still say, "I cannot realize that this is all compassion for me. I cannot believe that all this came of love for my soul." How then can God persuade you to believe in His lovingkindness?

3. Faith in Christ will give you peace. Of this you need not and I think you cannot have the least doubt. Are you then willing to receive the knowledge that God gave His Son for you *as individuals*? His own Word declares so. God, having raised up His Son, Jesus, sent Him to bless you in turning away every one of you from your iniquities. Therefore make no delay. Rouse up all the energies of your soul to this work—*at once*.

4. Sinners are not apt to distinguish between Christ given and Christ received. Christ given is one thing: Christ received is quite another. God has in great love given the donation: have you accepted it? It avails you nothing until you do. Believing on Him is accepting Him as given. For a long time you have known that the offer of Jesus as your Savior has been made to you. Have you cared anything about it? Have you had even *one* feeling of gratitude to express to God for His unspeakable gift? Have you ever uttered one *word* of gratitude? Have you ever come before God with the first note of thanksgiving? How does your ingratitude look even in your own eyes? And if you are ashamed of it yourself, how must you suppose it appears in the eyes of your Savior?

Suppose Jesus Christ were to come into this house while you are sitting here. You know by the halo of glory about His head that it can be none other than the Lord of glory whom you have so long rejected. He shows you the prints of the nails in His hands and feet—the wound of the spear in His side, and coming near where you sit, He asks you with a look of tenderest compassion, "Is all this nothing to you? Do you know who I am?" "Yes." "Do you know what I want of you?" "Yes." "Am I worthy of your confidence?" "I suppose so." "Then will you give yourself up to me, trusting my word and grace to save you and devoting yourself heartily to my cause?" "Oh," you answer, "I don't *feel* enough." "But," He replies, "I have come to save you. This matter has been debated long enough, and it is time you should tell me honestly what your final decision is. We must conclude this matter now, and whatever your decision may be, I shall write it down, and put the judgment seal upon it." And now under these circumstances, what will you do? Will you say, "Go thy way for this time"? "But if I do for this time, I return no more to bless you. I shall pray for you no more. All your day and scope for mercy will pass away. You know I have dealt in all honesty with you to save your soul if I can. I have sought to show you your enmity of heart against me, and have implored you to put it all away and give me your heart—will you do it even now, though it be your eleventh hour of mercy?"

Sinner, do you understand this appeal? Doubtless you do.

Christ is trying to win you. He would gladly persuade you to save your soul. Will you be persuaded? Will you decide the momentous question this hour? If you knew that your present decision would be final, what would it be? Let me tell you, *it may be final;* therefore, take care what you do! There is a point beyond which forbearance is no virtue, beyond which even God cannot forbear, for virtue forbids it. Remember, this is the dispensation of the Holy Spirit, and if you willfully sin against Him, He may never forgive you. But do you say, "The Holy Spirit is not now with me"? Beware what you say! Has not some influence other than your own mind convinced you of sin? Must you not admit that by some means you have seen your sins as you have rarely seen them before, and have been pressed to come to Christ for pardon? Then now is your time. You ought to consider that this may be your *last* time. Why then will you not cry out, "O Jesus take my heart. Oh, take it wholly and seal it thine forevermore!"[1]

---

[1]From *The Oberlin Evangelist*, June 23, 1852.

34

ON LOVING GOD

"Jesus replied, 'Love the Lord your God with all your heart and with all your soul and with all your mind. This is the first and greatest commandment'" (Matt. 22:37–38).

The connection in which this passage stands is striking. Our Savior was constantly engaged in rebuking the delusions and sophistries of the Sadduccees. In the times of our Savior, they were a sect of semi-infidels, rich and honored in the nation. On this occasion, Matthew remarks that when the Pharisees had heard that He had put the Saduccees to silence, they gathered about Him, and one of them, being a lawyer (not an attorney in our modern sense of lawyer, but a man who was skilled in the Mosaic law), asked Him a question, tempting Him, "Which is *the* great commandment of the law?"

To this question, Jesus promptly answered as in our text: "Thou shalt love the Lord thy God with all thy heart, and with all thy soul, and with all thy mind. This is the first and great commandment. And the second is like unto it, Thou shalt love thy neighbor as thyself. On these two commandments hang all the law and the prophets."

Notice how comprehensive our Lord makes His exposition of the fundamental law. All the books of Moses and the prophets hang upon it and are embraced within it. Indeed, everything written or unwritten, the entire preceptive part of religion is here. It covers the whole field of moral obligation to God and man.

It would require a whole course of lectures to discuss this subject fully. I propose only to touch briefly on some of its main points.

The kind of love required. You will readily see that this is a vital question. How can we hope to obey this first and great commandment unless we understand what it requires?

First, it must be a *volitional love*, not involuntary. This is shown plainly by the fact that it is required. Nothing but what is volitional can be properly demanded. The justice of God forbids Him to require and demand on pain of damnation anything that is beyond our power to do, that does not lie within the control of our volitional powers. This fundamental precept of the law cannot, therefore, be a thing of such sort that we have no volitional power to do it. In all reasonable law, every precept requires only volitional action; otherwise it is absurd.

An essential feature in the character of this love is that it must be *supreme*. The language used by our Lord very much implies this: "Thou shalt love with *all* thy heart and with *all* thy soul and with *all* thy mind."

Jesus commands us to have an *abiding love*. This love must be a *state* of goodwill, as distinguished from transient actions. A state of mind that is continuous must be implied and required in the commandment.

Some things implied in this love. If this love is goodwill—a perpetual purposing to promote the highest happiness of all—then it must imply a life devoted to this object. The love of the heart naturally and surely controls the life. Supreme love to God must therefore imply supreme devotion of the life to God, and by this I mean to pleasing God and faithfully doing all His known will. If love is supreme and abiding, it must forever control the life and hold it to perpetual devotion to the things that please God.

Here some will ask, "What can we do for God? Why should He care what we do?"

Ah, do you assume that God does not care what we do? Did God not care when those two young men shot down a father and mother in the field, and left their children orphans? To assume this would be to assume that God is no Father of His creatures at all.

Again, this law of love implies that we find our highest pleasure in seeking to know and do God's pleasure. If we have this love, it will be most grateful to us to please Him. It will be a richer joy to us to please God than to please ourselves. It will be our supreme pleasure to please God. We shall devote ourselves to pleasing Him and shall both seek and find our chief joy in this.

We sometimes see human beings so devoted to each other that they find their supreme pleasure in promoting each other's welfare. Obedience to this great law implies that such devotion should be toward God.

The exercise of this love implies a sympathy with whatever pleases God so that anything that anybody does to please God will surely please us. We shall naturally have a great satisfaction with anything that pleases God.

On the same principle, this love implies a state of mind that will be grieved with anything that displeases God. If we love God supremely, we shall account anything done against God as if it were done against ourselves. We would account it more painful than if it were done merely against ourselves.

Of course, it also implies that we are joyful in the exercise of self-denial for Christ's sake.

It sometimes happens that people receiving favors from us express so much gratitude that we are ready to thank them for the privilege of doing anything for them. See that little child sick and faint: she motions for a drink of water. Poor child; she can only lisp out, "Thank you, Mother!" Her mother did not need those uttered thanks. The grateful look sufficed. She so loved that dear sick child that it was joy enough for her to do anything for her welfare because of the love she bore. You have felt this. You have felt such love and such joy in doing any kindness to one you hold dear that you were ready to thank that one for the privilege of doing him any good. Your heart has been so set on doing good that you have felt it more blessed to give than to receive.

So God feels! God's love is of this very sort, pure good willing, pure love of doing all the good He can safely and wisely do for His children. His children feel so toward Him. If they can do anything for His cause, it is the highest joy of their heart. Suppose the Lord were to say to some of you, "You may do anything you please." Would you not at once reply, "Not so, Lord, but rather anything that pleases *you*"? Nothing else can ever please me except doing what pleases Him. What do I live for but to please and honor Him?

If you find one who cannot deny himself, but chooses his own ways to please himself rather than pleasing God, you know for certain He does not love God.

If you seek anyone's good with real love, you will certainly avail yourself of every means to learn what will please him. The same must be true of loving and pleasing God.

Of course supreme love implies a greater dread of displeasing God than anyone else. Nothing will distress one who loves God so much as the thought of displeasing Him.

You may apply every one of these principles warm and fresh to your own heart in self-examination. Say, "Does my love for God bear this out?"

If you truly love God, there will always be a spontaneous sorrow if you become conscious of having displeased Him. If you should be overcome by temptation, you would not need to make a great effort to feel sorry for it. When you have injured any friend whom you love more than any other being, you can easily regret and feel sorrow over the sad wrong.

When the heart is supremely engrossed with love for God, the thoughts will naturally turn toward Him. Where our treasure is, there will our heart be also.

Moreover, God will become the object of our complacent affections. The fact that He is infinitely lovely and good will secure in our hearts an intense satisfaction in His character, words and ways.

We shall find supreme satisfaction in His service. We always find the most satisfaction while pursuing the objects on which our affections are concentrated.

There will be a perpetual reference to God in all we do. Take the case of a man supremely devoted to his family. He will see everything in the light of its bearing on his family. So a father will do for his children if he supremely loves them. So a husband for his wife. Everything will be referred to the question of the happiness of the loved one. Thus real love for any friend produces spontaneous sympathy with him and with all his interests, and equally spontaneous sympathy *against* all his enemies.

What are the grounds of this obligation to God? The ground of our obligation is not that God has commanded it. We do not and cannot love merely out of regard to authority. God does not expect that His mere authority will produce and ensure love. But He bases His claim for our love on His own infinite worthiness, and on the infinite importance of having His creatures obey Him. The obligation to love God must always be equal to the value of God's happiness and glory, and to the good of His creatures as depending on His relations to them. To withhold due love from God is, therefore, to derogate from His rights and claims; and by consequence, from the rights and claims of the universe He has made and rules over to bless.

The natural consequences of refusing to render this supreme love and service to God. Refusing to love God will inevitably make you lose all true peace of mind. Every rational being is so constituted that he cannot be satisfied unless he gives God his heart's best love. He cannot have peace of mind and peace with God if he does not love God supremely. As long as this love is withheld, his soul will be uneasy and irritated because he is supremely selfish.

There are also governmental consequences for refusing to love God and serve Him supremely. God must condemn those who deny Him the love of their heart and the devotion of their life. He must regard them with holy displeasure. By all the love He bears to the best interests of His creatures, He must disown and be displeased with those who array themselves against Him and His great family. He is bound to reveal to all His creatures His displeasure against those who hate both Him and them. He ought to make the fact of this displeasure as manifest as He possibly can, for the happiness of the universe depends upon His revealing it most fully. He should make the revelations of His heart and of His hand against sin appropriate to what is right and just in each case as He can.

Consequently, God must make this revelation as enduring as His own government. Both the natural and governmental consequences of sin must be as enduring and as striking as God can make them. Otherwise, God cannot do justice to His responsibilities as the Great Moral Father of the universe.

Some delusions which prevail on this subject. People establish some standard of right. By a mutual consent or conventionalism, they make up a practical code of morals—morals in social life or in politics—and then take great credit to themselves for having done right.

Now let people devise their own codes and notions as they may. Still, this law of God is forevermore the one and only great standard of right. Nothing is right unless it is in accordance with this law. If people talk about doing right, on any rule of right short of this, they grievously deceive themselves. What do you mean by "doing right"? Do you mean that your life is a constant offering to God? Do you offer yourself to God as a living sacrifice? If not, why do you talk about pleasing God? Do you say, "I pay all my debts; I live fairly in society; I injure no man"?

Suppose you were doing no wrong to your neighbor, yet your relationship to God was not right. If you care nothing for God, what is this but wishing to dethrone God, denying His right to reign, and denying His parental love and care over all His creatures?

Imagine a band of robbers, outlaws against all human governments. They may have what they are pleased to call excellent rules among themselves. They may treat each other with great kindness. When they have rushed out of their stronghold and come down upon some lovely, quiet village, burned down their houses, murdered whoever resists, and plundered them of everything they care for, they go back and divide the booty perhaps very honorably among each other. They are careful to provide for their sick, and they take great interest in training themselves in dexterity and skill, so as to rob and murder with the best success.

Now, what of all the good and right things in these bandits? What would you think of them if they were to justify themselves before the bar of mankind by appealing to their kindness to each other, their justice to each other, and their great diligence in caring for everything that would make them good and successful robbers?

In the same way all sinners are outlaws with regard to God and His Kingdom. They have their own ways and choose none of His. Regarding their efforts toward God, their whole spirit is transgression; just as a band of robbers exist on the principle of setting at nought all human governments and abjuring all obligation to seek or to respect the welfare of their fellow human beings outside of their own group of robbers.

A gang of these outlawed freebooters, if arrested and brought before a court of justice, might be very apt to say, if they dared, "Why, what evil have we done?" Naturally, if they chance to escape they will go back to their comrades and appeal to them, "Have not we done right? Are not we all good fellows?" To which the whole band of robbers would respond, "First rate; all noble and true—generous fellows!"

This would be farce to play before the face of the civilized world!

Suppose a pirate ship should be fitted up with her black flag and skull and bones, and with her brave buccaneers and their cannons, and then boast of being the best managed ship on the seas. Nowhere, say they, can you find seamen so experienced, so brave, so faithful to their commander. Nowhere else are officers so daring and so true.

But what commendations are these to pirates? Do they sanctify the guilty business of piracy?

But the pirate may still ask: "What have I done?" Pause and see what. Just what the selfishness and wickedness of your heart has prompted: nothing else, nothing better. Men could do nothing in the pirate's business without these virtues. Those, therefore, who choose a pirate's life must pay at least so much homage to virtue as to be truthful, kind and generous to each other. And then they shall be blind enough to plead in self-defense that they are very moral pirates, very kind and true to one another, and very much devoted to their business!

Like the self-justifying pirate, so the sinner asks, "What have I done?" Done? You have waged war against God and all the nations of men. And can you call that doing right? Will you plead that you are trying to do right?

It is a very simple thing to examine yourself and to know whether you are right before God and His law. Is it your great aim to please God? Is it the business of your life? What have you done today to learn His will and to do His pleasure? Have you given yourself to prayer and to the faithful study of His Word? Have you been seeking in all possible ways to please and honor your Father in heaven? Have you not been adorning yourself to display your beauty? Or is it true that you really bathe yourself in His presence all the day long and deem yourself blest then and then only when you have the consciousness of pleasing Him?

"Be not deceived; God is not mocked; whatever a man soweth, that shall he also reap" (Gal. 6:7).[1]

[1]From *The Oberlin Evangelist*, June 20, 1860.

35

ON LOVE TO OUR NEIGHBOR

"And the second is like unto it; Thou shalt love thy neighbor as thyself" (Matt. 22:34).

In speaking upon this portion of our Lord's epitome of the divine law, I will:

    I. *Show what kind of love is required in this verse;*
   II. *Show some of the things implied in this love;*
  III. *Show that nothing short of this is true humanity;*
  IV. *Show that nothing short of this is true morality.*

I. *Show what kind of love is required in this verse.*

The love required toward our neighbor is certainly not complacency in his character. Complacency is approbation and delight in character, but our Lord makes no distinction between the good and the bad in this commandment. Therefore, He requires us to love them all. It cannot be that He requires us to approve and delight in the character of bad people; hence, we must conclude that the love of complacency is not in His mind, and is not the thing He requires. To have complacency in the character of wicked people as *wicked* is to be as bad as they are. This is something no reasonable person can suppose to be what the Savior requires, or what He interprets the law of God to require.

God does not require the love of fondness, which we sometimes feel toward particular individuals. Some people are nat-

195

urally pleasing to certain other people. Some are pleasing to all, since they are naturally amiable and adapted to awaken pleasing emotions. But this is not the love referred to in the text.

This love that God requires cannot be involuntary. As I said before of the love required toward God, it must be a volitional act and could not be involuntary because if it were, it could not be justly demanded. So I say the same thing regarding love to our neighbor. It cannot be involuntary, for if it were, no just being could require it.

Positively, this love to our neighbor is and must be goodwill. God's love to us is goodwill—a pure and strong interest in our welfare, a desire for our happiness, and the positive willing of our happiness as the object dearest to His heart. The way in which His great love has manifested itself proves this. Our very reason affirms that this is the love God has borne and now bears to our race. Consequently, we must conclude that this is the love which He requires us to exercise toward each other.

Note again that this love requires us to esteem our neighbor's interests as our own. This rule applies to all our neighbors—to our enemies as well as to our friends.

Finally, this love must be a constant love. It cannot be sporadic and short-lived, or impulsive. It must flow from a fountain of goodwill that is ever enduring. It is a state of mind—an *established* state which regards our neighbors' interest as our own.

II. *Show some of the things implied in this love.*

It does not imply the universal and equal distribution of our energies and means among all the human race, or even among all those who may be near enough to be known to us personally. It cannot mean to imply this, because with such a meaning it would be impossible to obey it.

There can be no doubt that the law of God demands goodwill toward all mankind, always, under all circumstances; but there are circumstances which forbid such modes of expressing it as would be proper at other times. A criminal, suffering the just sentence of human law, must not receive from us the same acts of goodwill as would be fitting after his sentence is served out, or if he were not under sentence at all. The relation which sinners come to sustain toward God under the sentence of His law is such as forbids Him to bless them. It is not that He has ceased to love them, in the sense of a deep, intense interest in their happiness. But He loves all the rest of His intelligent creatures no less, and their interest demand of Him that He should execute His righteous law against the wicked. Hence, He cannot give them even so much good as a cup of cold water.

The same circumstances may sometimes demand of us the same withholding of positive efforts to do good to the wicked.

Since each person is required by this law to love his neighbor, it is plain that God intends that these kind actions should be mutual. If God does us good, we should gratefully seek to do Him good. If He promotes our interests, we should strive to promote His.

So of children toward their parents. Children should not always receive and never give, but should account it a great privilege to repay their parents for the labor and care bestowed on them. When parents live long and become old and helpless, their children should rejoice in the opportunity to repay the favors shown them when they too were helpless.

The same should be true of subjects and rulers. So between pupils and teachers, there are reciprocal interests. On neither side should it be all receiving and not giving, but there should be mutual receiving and giving on both sides.

In like manner, this institution [Oberlin College], including its teachers and its students, sustains close relationships to its founders and patrons. Others have labored. We enter into their labors. Others have given their money, and we are enjoying the benefit. There is not a building here that is not indebted to some donors abroad. Others have prayed, and we have received blessings from God for those prayers.

Hence, we should seek to repay those favors, doing all we can to promote the very goals to which those Christian friends have so devoted their wealth and their prayers.

So ministers who preach and their people who hear should be mutually giving and receiving good to and from each other.

All of us, instead of being merely recipients of good from others, should strive to do good to others also, rendering back to them liberally.

Why shouldn't this principle apply to all people in this attitude toward God? You who have never cared for God: is it right that you should receive everything from God and make no returns of love and obedience to Him? Have you no zeal for His honor and no devotion to His interests? He has nourished and brought you up as a child, and you have done nothing else but rebel against Him. Is that right? Why should you not rather say, "God has given me talents and I must render back to Him in their use as I may have opportunity"? Certainly you must regard God as your neighbor in the sense that He has interests and rights, and you are under the highest obligations to repay Him for His numerous favors.

The same is true also of your relationship to the church of Jesus Christ. How much do you owe to Him? In view of it all, have you any right to say, "Not one word of acknowledgment, not one thank-offering shall He ever have from me"? What do you not owe Him? Has it ever occurred to you how you really owe Him your very existence, since but for His mission of mercy, you would have never lived? Except for that offering and sacrifice on Calvary, none of us could have had any existence at all. But for that, Adam and Eve must have been cut down at once in their sin, the law taking its course of righteous judgment—"In the day thou eatest thereof thou shalt surely die" (Gen. 2:17). You live, therefore, only because God has had mercy on our race. Come now, rise up at once to meet the claims of this great truth. Are you not indebted to God for everything? And will you pay back absolutely nothing? Here you are in the house of God, surrounded with an atmosphere of prayer, instead of being in hell, shrieking and wailing in the depths of despair!

Do you say, "I don't owe Christ anything"? But you profess to be respectable. Yet who can respect you if you treat Jesus Christ this way? Have you no sympathy with His great sacrifices and sufferings to save you? Would you leave all the labor and sacrifice for Him, and make no response of love or gratitude? Will you utterly refuse to love Him? Do you say, "He is welcome to love me and to die for me; but I have nothing to pay Him in return? I leave it for Him to do and to suffer all, and not a word of thanks can He have from me"? Do you think this is right? Is it generous? Ought it to be deemed respectable?

III. *Show that nothing short of this love is true humanity.*

It is not true humanity to do good only to your own offspring. They are regarded as part of your own self, and hence doing good only to them is nothing beyond a slightly enlarged selfishness. Nothing is really love to man—true humanity—except that love which estimates human well-being for its intrinsic value, and loves man as man.

IV. *Show that nothing short of this is true morality.*

Nothing less than this love for neighbor is required by our reason and our conscience. To lay special stress on our own interests because they are our own is not true morality. It is not, even though we aim to be honest in seeking the good of particular individuals. If it is only special individuals that we love, this is partiality.

No one loves his friends in the sense that pleases God unless he also truly loves his enemies. Suppose a person does love his friends. Hear what Jesus Christ says precisely of this case: "If ye love them who love you, what reward have ye? Do not even publicans [notorious sinners] the same?" Jesus Christ says, "Love your enemies." It can never be supposed that one does right unless he loves his enemies.

Someone says, "There are certain people to whom I never do anything wrong." What is the motive leading you to do them good and not evil? If you truly loved your neighbor for right reasons, you would love every neighbor, and you would take every living person for your neighbor in the sense of this law. You would love every known being . . . because you would love to promote the happiness of all cognizant existences, and you would aim to love each one according to the value of his well-being. Real benevolence would as truly seek to do good to enemies as to friends, if it could reach them, and do them as much good. Understand, that to love your friend rightly, you must love him as God does, and for the same reasons. You cannot love him rightly unless you love your enemies also and for a similar reason. No one does anything for his friend which would be acceptable to God unless he would do as much for his enemies if he could. God can give him no credit for doing good to his friends unless he does it on a principle which would make him do as much for his enemies if he could. No one does any duty acceptable to God for one man while he refuses or willfully neglects to do the same for another. And this I put on the ground that God's law requires you to love *all* your neighbors—every neighbor; and if you have the spirit of obedience to God, you will.

No one does right in any proper sense who does not act from universal and disinterested love. On any other ground it cannot be acceptable for one moment. That mother nursing her baby has no credit from God for this if she does it on no higher principle than the mere animal. She is bound to love her own children because God has placed her in precisely those relations. But let her by no means think she has any credit from God for obeying merely her animal instincts. Her soul should go higher than the mere animal. She is bound to study to please God.

Nothing short of his love can be the condition of salvation. No one can be out of sin and in grace who is not brought into a state of true love to his neighbor. What would become of a person applying at heaven's gate for admittance, who should there meet an enemy—a person he had never loved, whom he had hated and never prayed for? Could he pass by such a person on his way into heaven?

How could you enjoy heaven without a holy heart? Some of you would hasten out as we have sometimes seen rude, unmannered boys rush to get out of church, even before the services of worship were closed. He who loves his neighbor will understand that it is one of his neighbor's rights to enjoy the public worship of God without being disturbed.

Without this love, salvation is naturally impossible. It is governmentally impossible. It cannot be, as long as God rules and cares for the interests of His great kingdom. The entrance to heaven is so guarded all round about that nothing shall by any means enter that works abomination—nothing unholy. Shall a person go to heaven in his selfishness? Not if God can keep him out!

REMARKS

If everyone obeyed the laws of God, society would be perfect. I do not mean that there would be no further progress, no advance, no improvement; no, not this, for much remains to be done. But it is true that morality would be perfect. There would be no more war and strife. Every family would be a little emblem of heaven. Every community would bear the image of heaven. The wings of angels would come down so near they would fan such loving hearts, and heaven's doors would stand open all day long before such a people.

We see how we are to treat those who are oppressed and in slavery. We are to put ourselves in their position and inquire what we should ask them to do for us, in their circumstances. Suppose my family and I were in slavery. Election time is approaching. Have I a right to expect my friends in Ohio to cast their votes so as to bear directly upon my liberation? I should be very prone to think that no one ought to cast his vote against my liberty for the mere sake of money or office. Even politicians can see how shameful and how outrageously wrong it is to hold any person as a slave. That slavery should be deemed an institution sanctioned by the Bible is of all horrible things most monstrous! It is so revolting that I cannot imagine how anybody can be honest in holding this opinion. Yet let us be candid: I can easily see that the merely legal relation may exist without any violation of the law of love.

This golden rule is equally applicable everywhere and in all circumstances. It is good when applied in the matter of asking favors. We ought not to ask a favor of any man when a knowledge of his circumstances and a proper sympathy for his welfare, such as we would have him feel for ours, would forbid it.

The same is true of receiving favors. This law, honestly applied, would show us what favors we should be willing to allow others to do for us. Sometimes we cannot properly allow others to do us favors. If a poor man has labored for me a month and refuses to receive compensation, I too must by all means refuse to receive his labor as a gift. A proper regard to his circumstances compels me to refuse so great a gift from him. He cannot afford to give it; therefore, I cannot afford to receive it.

You may see from this subject what the morality of unregenerate men is. It is not morality at all, in any just sense. All their morals are only sin.

You may also see God's personal relations to selfishness. Every particle of selfishness is personally hostile and hateful to God. It is so utterly unlike His heart, so totally opposed to all His principles and to all His acts, He can have no fellowship with it. He must forever hold it in utter abhorrence.

You may also see His governmental relations to sin. He can hear the personal insult and He does—does for the time, and, but for governmental reasons, would pass it over perhaps forever. He endures with sinners now. He does not fret; does not manifest excited passion, as people do under insult; but the governmental bearings of sin He cannot overlook. The selfishness of people toward Him and toward each other, He must see. He is a magistrate bearing the highest responsibilities of the universe. All eyes are turned upon Him. He must mark the iniquities that are done among His subjects and His creatures. He must see all their wickedness, biting and devouring one another, trampling each other down. All eyes are upturned toward Him. What says the Judge of all the earth to this! Ah, this must be answered! God's relations to His government make it an awful thing for anyone to love selfishness.

Every selfish sinner is in certain peril of eternal death. People cannot but know this. God's mercy flows at your feet—a deep, broad, glorious current; yet you heed it not! Yet you thrust Jesus away! You have done it so often and for so long. Can you do it yet longer? Jesus, with bleeding heart and loving hand, is pressing near to save you, but you are saying, "Depart from me! Leave me alone in my sins yet longer! I will not have this man to rule over me, nor to save me, on such terms of salvation!"

Oh sinner, will you still pursue a course so ruinous and so outrageously abusive to Jesus Christ![1]

---

[1]From *The Oberlin Evangelist*, July 4, 1860.